JRC
CW01655296

JACK PENDER
A Tribute

Frank Ruhrmund

Introduction by Alison Bevan
Director, Penlee House Gallery and Museum, Penzance

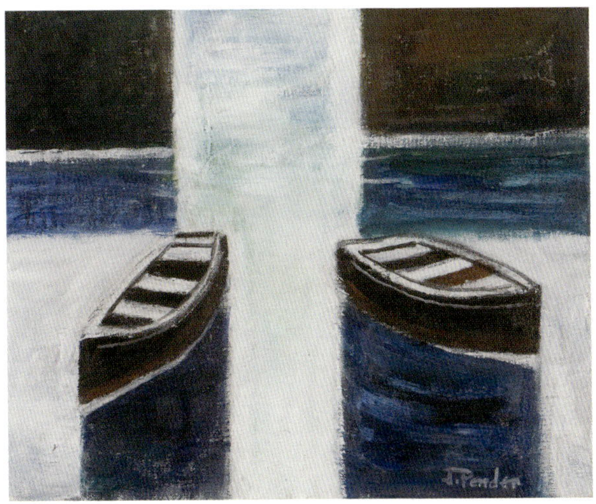

Untitled, c1970's, oil on canvas

truran

Published by Truran, Croft Prince, Mount Hawke,
Truro, Cornwall TR4 8EE
www.truranbooks.co.uk

Truran is an imprint of Truran Books Ltd

ISBN 978 185022 220 0

Text © Frank Ruhrmund 2008
Intoduction © Alison Bevan 2008
Cover image, all illustrations and family photographs © Pender family
All colour photographs of paintings by Vince Bevan except Tony Hutchings pp42, 44, 45, 48
Back Cover photograph © Phil Monckton

Printed and bound in Cornwall by R. Booth Ltd,
The Praze, Penryn, TR10 8AA

Front Cover: *Self-portrait, c1940's, oil on board*
Back Cover: *Frank Ruhrmund and Jack Pender, both Cornish Bards, on one of their frequent forays to the Cornish Gorsedd, Marazion 1990* © Phil Monckton
Inside Front Cover: *Early Sun, c1960's, oil on board*
Inside Back Cover: *Winter Morning, c1980's, acrylic on board*

My thanks to all thosewho assisted with the publication, particularly the members of the Pender family: Madeleine, Robin, Jason, Tamsin and Sylvia, and David Lay.
Published to coincide with the exhibition *Jack Pender*, at Penlee House Gallery and Museum, Penzance, sponsored by David Lay.

DAVID LAY FRICS

PENLEE HOUSE
Gallery & Museum
PENZANCE

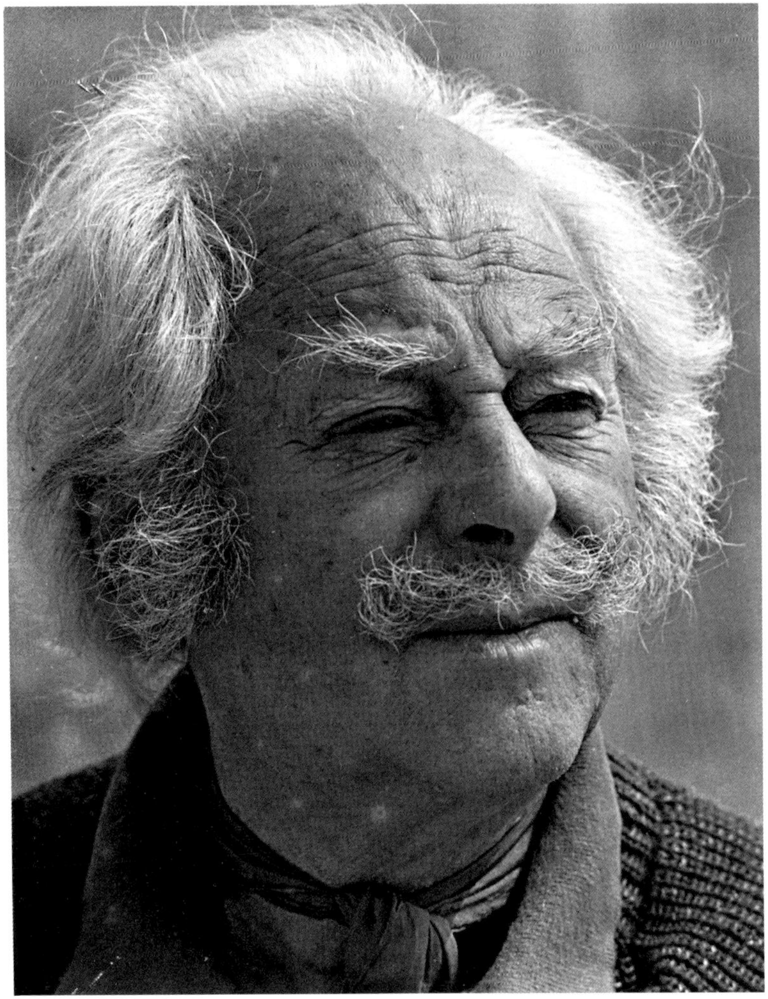

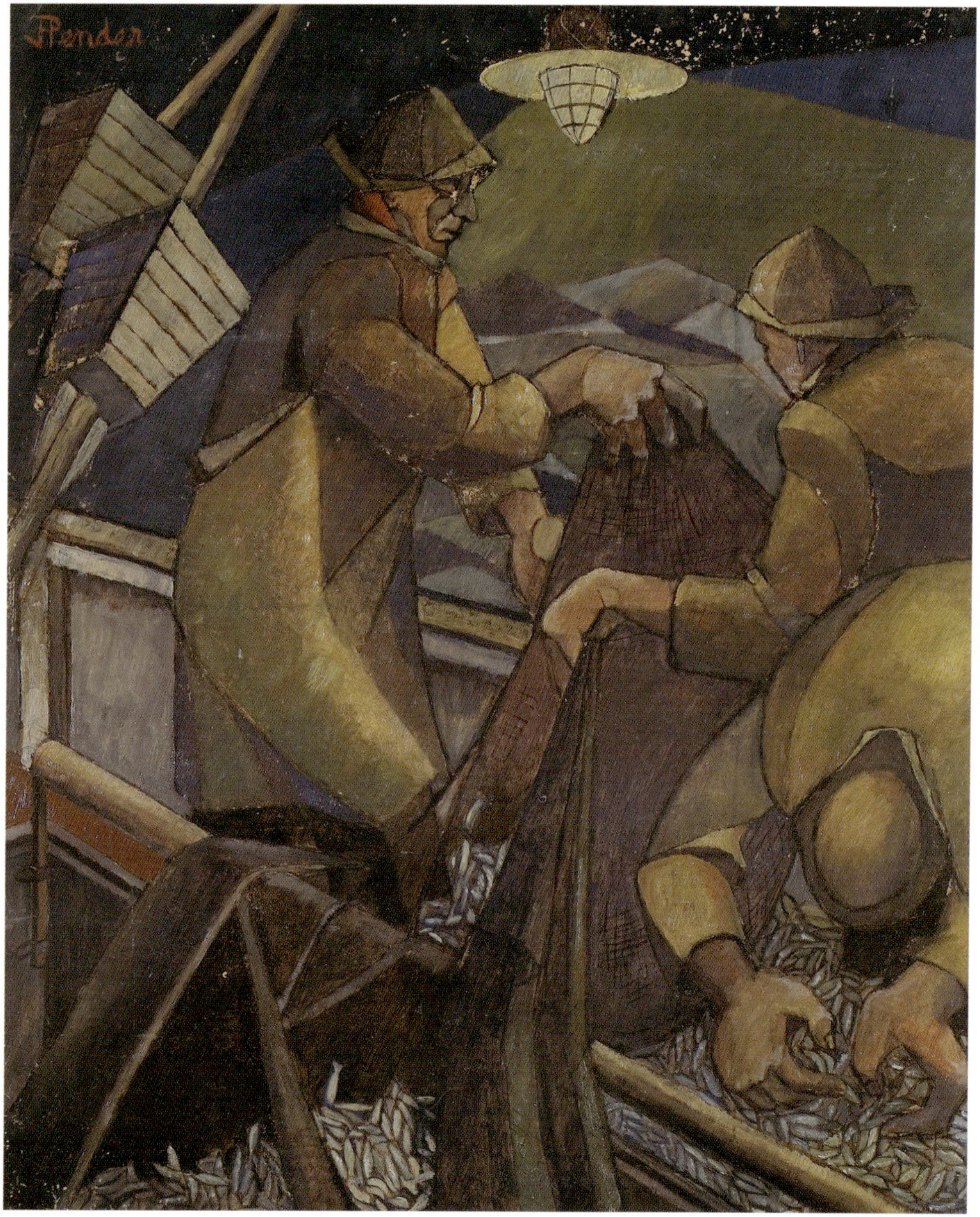

Untitled, c1940's, oil on board

Introduction

As Director of Penlee House, I have been lucky enough to gain entry into the homes of some of the most distinguished private collectors of Cornish art. Among many collections are I noticed one or two stunning works which, at first, I could not recognise as being by any of the established canon of Newlyn or St Ives artists; on enquiring who they were by, I'd be told 'Oh, that's a Jack Pender'. These Pender works not only hold an equal place in the collectors' affections, but thoroughly stand up to the company they are in, and encountering them signalled to me a need to bring this painter to wider acclaim.

Born anywhere other than West Cornwall, Pender's talent would surely have shone out, but for a Mousehole-man to gain recognition, encircled by some of the greatest artists of his age, was a challenging task. His being, in all senses, a 'popular local artist' – a phrase that often seems to engender disrespect among the art establishment – has perhaps further hampered Pender's national reputation. As his inclusion in Tate London's 1985 St Ives show demonstrates, however, meaningful recognition of Pender's work has not been entirely lacking, but it has been sporadic, and it is surely now time to place him permanently among the leading Cornish painters.

Like many 20th century artists, Jack Pender's influences were many and varied. His first inspiration probably came from his maternal grandfather, William George, whose remarkable naïve landscapes (produced during the last 19 years of his life up to his death at 94) are imbued with something of the energy and singular vision Jack was to develop. Jack's, story of watching Christopher Wood paint in Mouseholewhen he was a boy was probably apocryphal, but Wood was clearly an influence, as he was on so many others. More importantly, the professionalism and commitment of west Cornwall's resident and visiting artists fuelled his dedication to art.

A leading member of the Newlyn Society of Artists in the 1950s, Pender was part of the core exhibiting group with Lanyon, Mackenzie, Tunnard, Wells, Weschke and Wynter, among others,

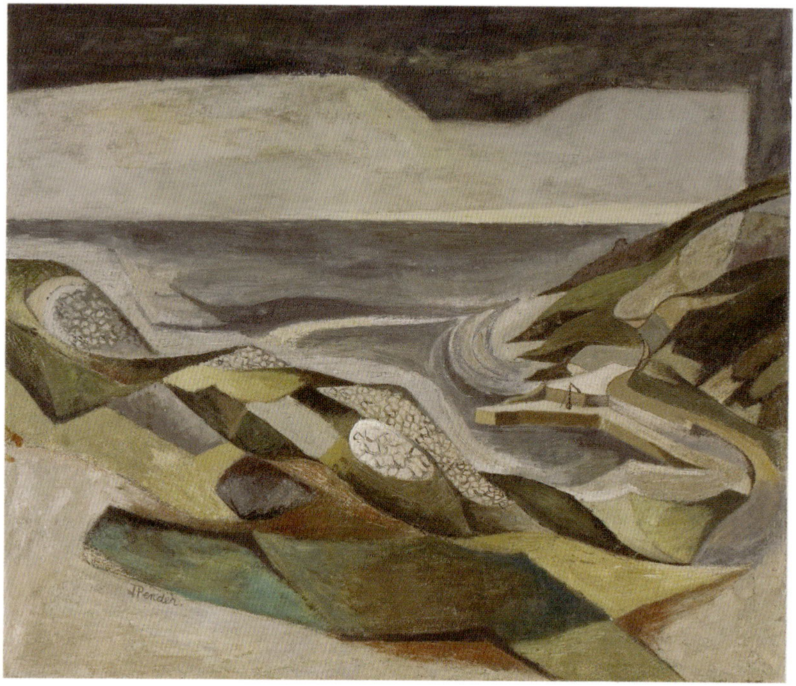

Lamorna, c1950's, oil on board

and shared influences often lead to hints of one-another's style. Pender was also an early member of the Penwith Society, formed when the 'Crypt Group' of modernists split from the traditionalists of the St Ives Society of Artists, and he joined their Committee in the 1960s. The abstracted simplification of shapes in Pender's work shows shared modernist leanings, yet the vestiges of traditional objectivity remained at the core of his work. As his son, Robin, puts it "his best works reinterpret what he saw about him, making what he painted resonate for the viewer, capturing the juxtaposition of boats and cottages, fishermen and nets. He spoke of finding the essence of a boat, not to just make a pictorially accurate representation of one. Jack's boats have personality."

Pender was a painter of great energy and drive, and despite occasional fallow periods, he was extremely prolific over the course of his career. This book gives a glimpse of the sheer breadth of his work, through its many changes of style. It is telling that after two successful one-man shows at the Arnolfini Gallery, Bristol, in the late sixties, he declined their offer to be his agent, later telling Robin that he had done so because he did not want to be pigeon-holed and forced to paint in a certain way. He continued to experiment throughout his career, but also returned to styles and themes, sometimes reworking earlier paintings, or adding to a series years later. His own voice remains clear throughout the stylistic variations, however, and his virtuoso handling of his medium gives a delicious painterly quality across his ouvre.

A decade after his death, Jack Pender is still remembered with huge affection: he was clearly a

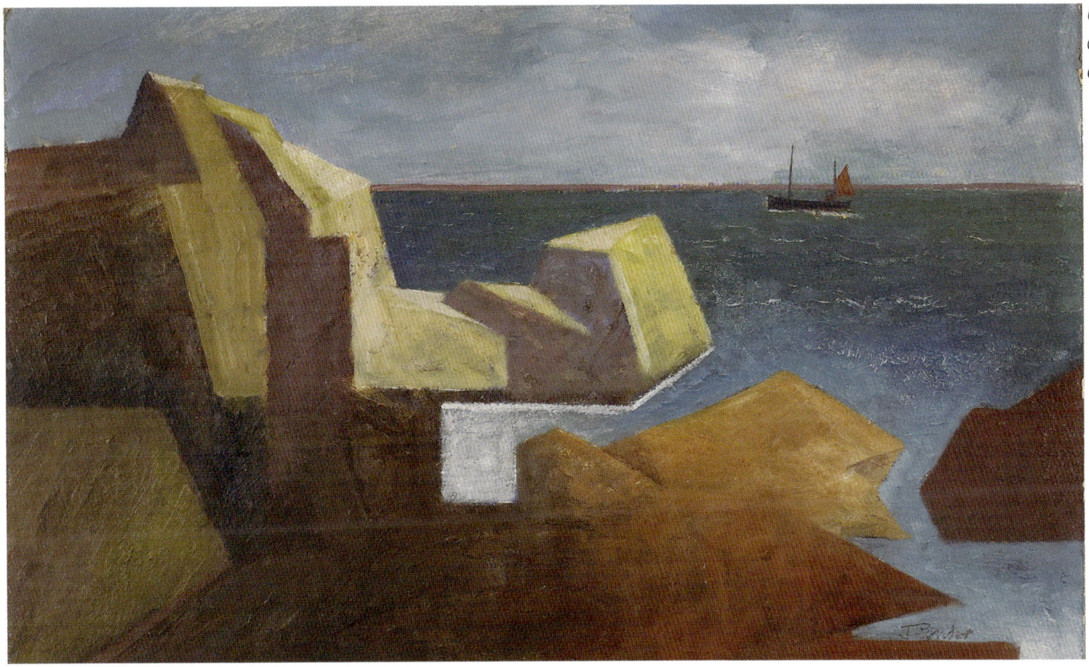

Untitled, c1970's, oil and/or acrylic on board

great character whose ebullient personality left an indelible mark. For those, like me, who never knew the man himself, it is purely the sincerity and the integrity of his vision that shines through, testified to by a vast and exceptional body of work.

This book, and the exhibition which accompanied its launch, could not have happened without the generous support of many owners of Pender's work. We are grateful, too, to our sponsor, David Lay FRICS, and to Frank Ruhrmund for his excellent text. Finally, greatest thanks must go to the artist's children, Robin, Jason and Tamsin, who have been unstinting in their assistance and encouragement: the result is a testament to them, as well as to their father.
Alison Bevan,
Director, Penlee House Gallery & Museum, Penzance

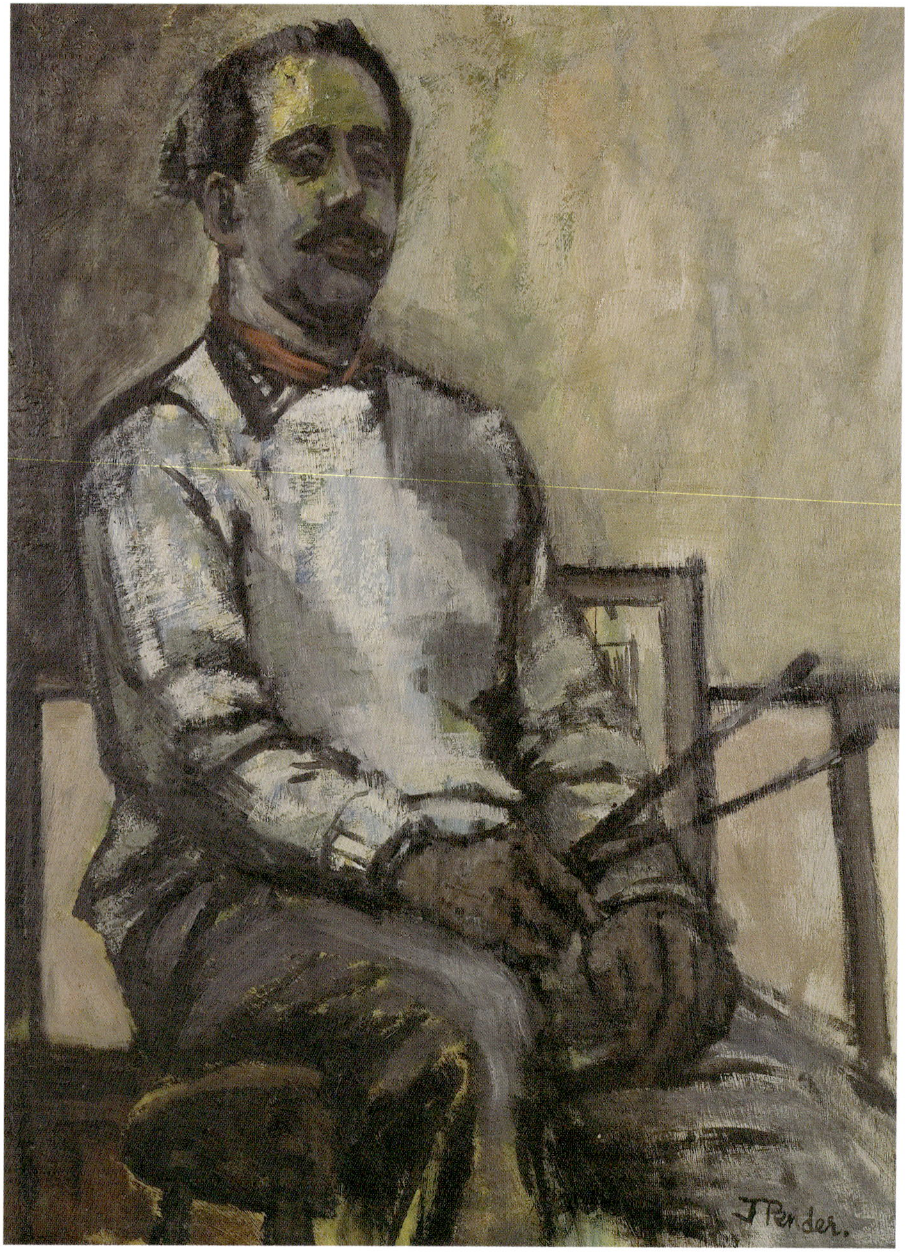

Self-Portrait, c1950's, oil on board

Preface

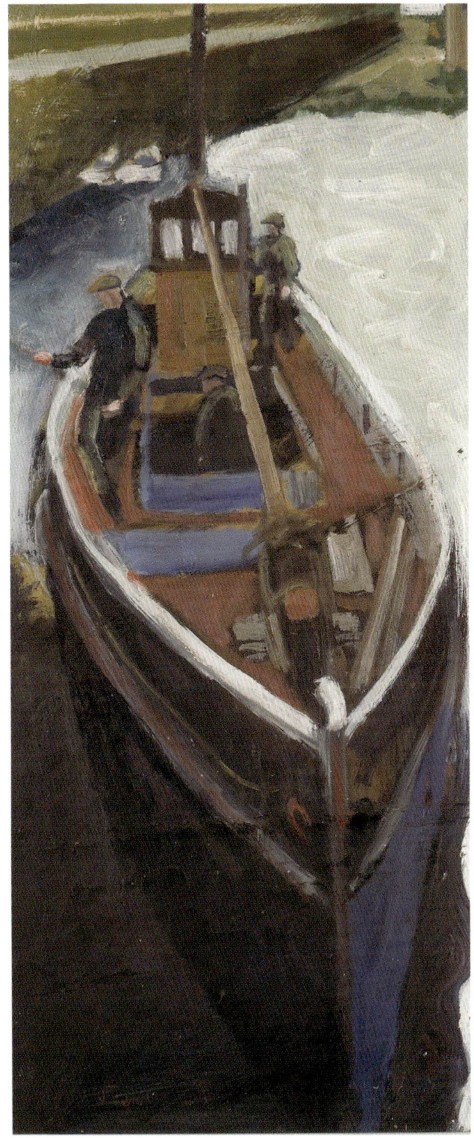

Back Home

Jack died in Bristol in June 1998, only hours before the marriage of his second son Jason and a few days after having celebrated his 80th birthday. For me and, I suspect for a host of others as well, Mousehole has never been quite the same since.

I had the privilege of giving the eulogy at his funeral service in St. Clement's Methodist Church, Mousehole, a duty which Jack had asked, or rather commanded, me to carry out for him several years before. While I can no longer remember what prompted such a request, I do recall agreeing while questioning why he had asked me rather than anyone else, whereupon, rubbing his hands together as he did when particularly pleased, he replied, "It's the thought of a Newlyn man coming round the Point to stand in the pulpit and sing the praises of a Mousehole man which appeals to me!" We had kept up this historic rivalry, even enmity, between the inhabitants of Mousehole and Newlyn as a running joke ever since we had worked together in the 1970's, Jack doing the drawings, me writing the words, for "Penwith Poems" an act described as "an unholy alliance between a Mousehole Cut-throat and a Newlyn Bucca".

Shortly before he left for Bristol he reminded me of that request or command, adding: "And whatever else you say or do on the day, boy, make sure you make 'em laugh." In return I must have expressed some doubts about my ability to do that, as he immediately came back with, "Of course you will, after all, everybody from Newlyn is a comedian."

Could he be here now, I'm certain be would be rubbing his hands together at the thought of me being asked to write this book about him to accompany his tribute exhibition. Just what he would have to say about it is anybody's guess, but he would probably come up with something to the effect that it's typical of a Newlyn man to begin at the end. By way of explanation rather than justification, I must state that I have done so deliberately as I want to make it clear from the word go that, whatever else this may be, it is not an objective but subjective account of the life and times of the painter Jack Pender. I'm proud to say we were close friends, and only too happy to admit that, while I've tried to remain as fair and balanced as possible in all that follows, if there is a bias then it will always be in Jack's favour.

Proposed Mural for Ministry of Agriculture and Fisheries, c1940's, gouache on paper

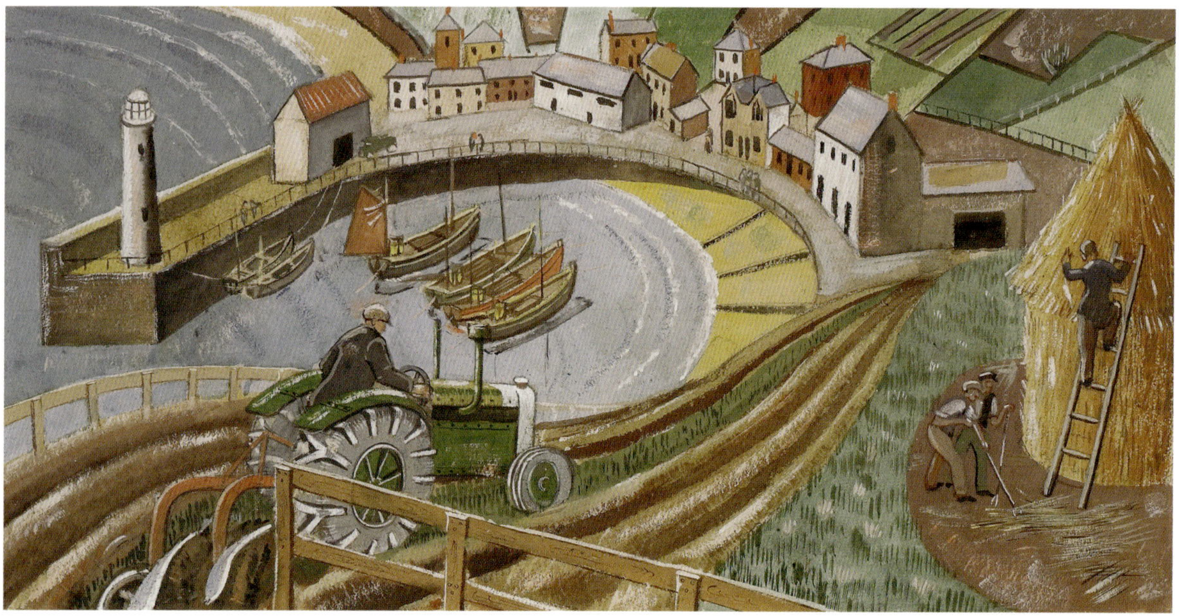

1 Early Years

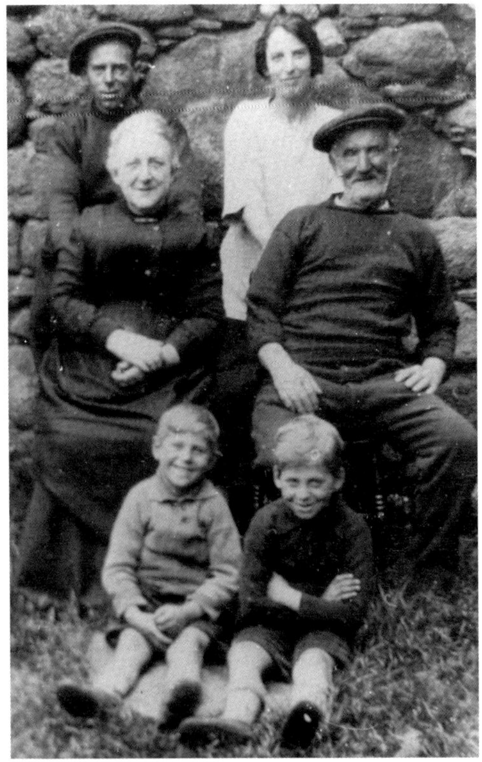

Three generations of the Pender family. Bill and Jack, their grandparents (grandpa Will George), and their parents Nettie and John Pender

Born on June 1, 1918, Jack grew up during the 1920's and 30's in a Mousehole which, although already beginning to change, was still a village in which most of its inhabitants, like him, had also been born and bred there, a place in which everyone knew everyone else, where you could safely leave your door unlocked day or night, and where fish were still more plentiful and more important than tourists. While its harbour may not have been as tightly packed with boats as it had once been, when it was possible to walk across the harbour from deck to deck, it was still a working port and among the many boats fishing from there was that of his father's, the "Lyonesse" PZ 81. A boat which was to play a considerable role in Jack's life, he was to use it so often as subject matter in his paintings that, when a student at art college, he was given the nickname of "PZ 81". He would later go to sea for a season and work on her alongside his father – a period he often referred to as one in which he discovered what hard work was all about.

Member of a deeply-rooted Mousehole family, his mother Nettie was a descendant of John Wills, one of those involved in the erection of a quay there in the 14th century, and the family home is less than a stone's throw away from where the celebrated Dolly Pentreath once lived. Jack attended the village school and from there went to Penzance School of Art where, incidentally, one of his fellow students was Peter Lanyon. Determined to be an artist for as long as he could

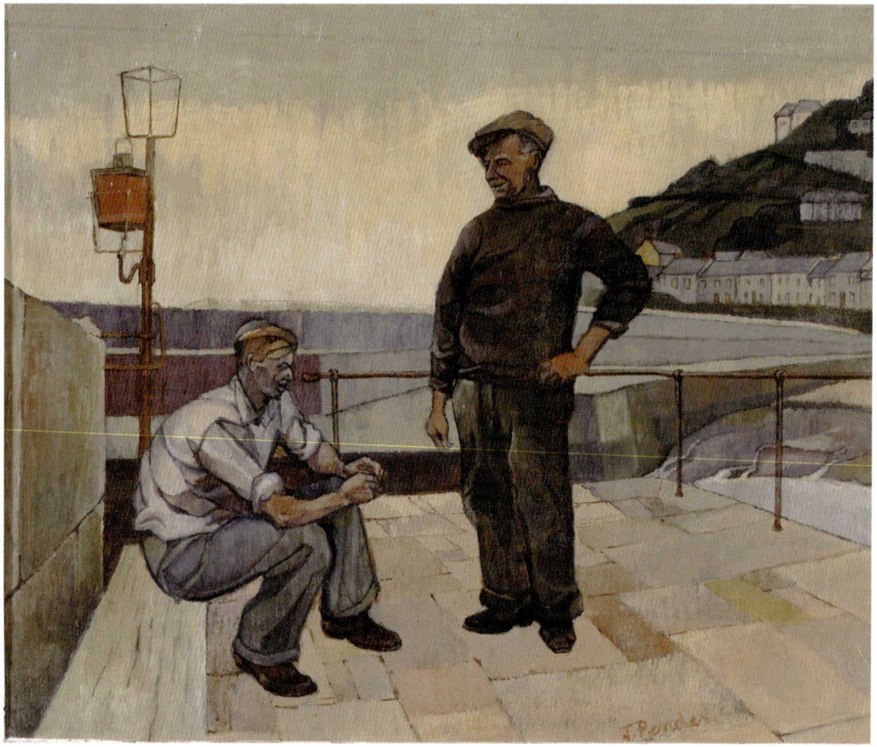

Conversation, 1950, oil on board

remember, while it has been suggested that Jack's experience, when only 12 years old, of having watched Christopher Wood paint his celebrated "PZ134" in Mousehole, helped inspire him to become a painter, it is likely that his future as an artist owed more to his grandfather W.J. (Will) George than to anyone else.

Jack loved him and wrote a most moving word portrait of him, published in Denys Val Baker's "The Cornish Review" in 1971. A piece so well written it suggested that Jack, had he so wished, could have been as accomplished with his pen as he was with his paintbrush.

"He lived with us, or we with him...he started to paint at the age of 75, between then and his death in 1945 at the age of 94, he produced countless works, intricate in design and detail and of great quality." Describing one of his grandfather's paintings, he says, "Three black boats, brown mizzen sails steadying, white foam creaming their bows, past the reaching arms of their home harbour, past the protecting island that forms a natural break-water to the one-time busy fishing village of Mousehole. The urgency of their progress is witnessed, felt and recorded."

"A gentle philosopher, fisherman and painter, he knew the urgency, labour, hardship and danger of the fisherman's life from the age of nine. At ten he was journeying in a 40ft Mount's Bay sailing lugger in search of herring. First to Ireland, on to Scotland, through the Caledonian Canal to the North Sea, down the East coast to Scarborough, Yarmouth, Plymouth and home. Four weary months as cook, bottle washer, and general factotum to five Cornish fishermen." Speaking of his grandfather in his later life, he says, "His real thirst for enlightenment, knowledge, experience, beauty and joy through the medium of the written word was never satiated. He remembered, thought, theorised and taught. Many were the strange "up country gentry" with unfamiliar accents who found their way to our small living room to sit and chat with him."

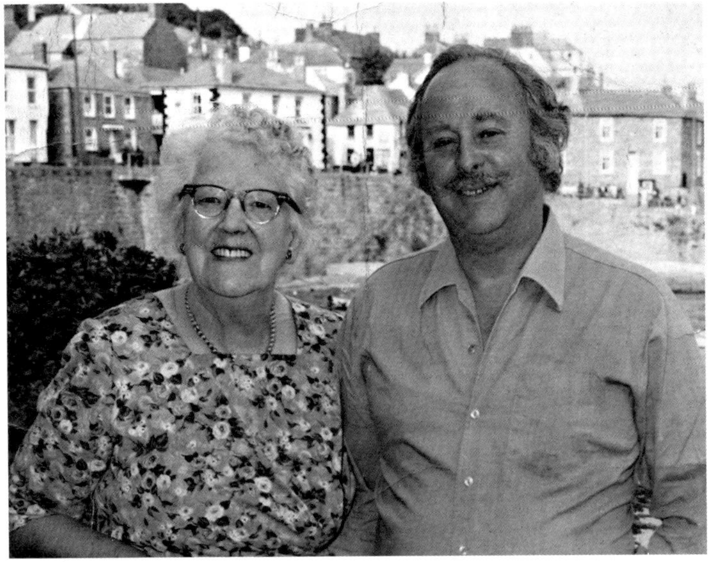
Jack with his mother Nettie

As a painter Will George was "discovered" by the Penwith artist Alethea Garstin. "She introduced his work to the Passmore Edwards Art Gallery in Newlyn and to the painters of the area. On sunny afternoons she sometimes drove him about the countryside and to her home, in Zennor, for tea. From that time artists from this country and abroad made their way to the small cottage. Few left without buying a painting for the price of an ounce of "baccy", all he asked for. His paintings hang in homes all over the world and a great number still remain in Mousehole, where it was the custom to ask him for a painting to be given as a wedding present."

Something quite similar would later happen to many of Jack's own paintings. Encouraged by his parents, Jack thoroughly enjoyed his time at Penzance School of Art. No one was more aware of the hazards of fishing than his father and the chance that his son's training at art school would lead to something more settled and safer must have had considerable appeal, while for his mother, with whom he had a very close relationship, it must have been an even greater comfort. Unfortunately, such seeming security was shattered by the start of the Second World War.

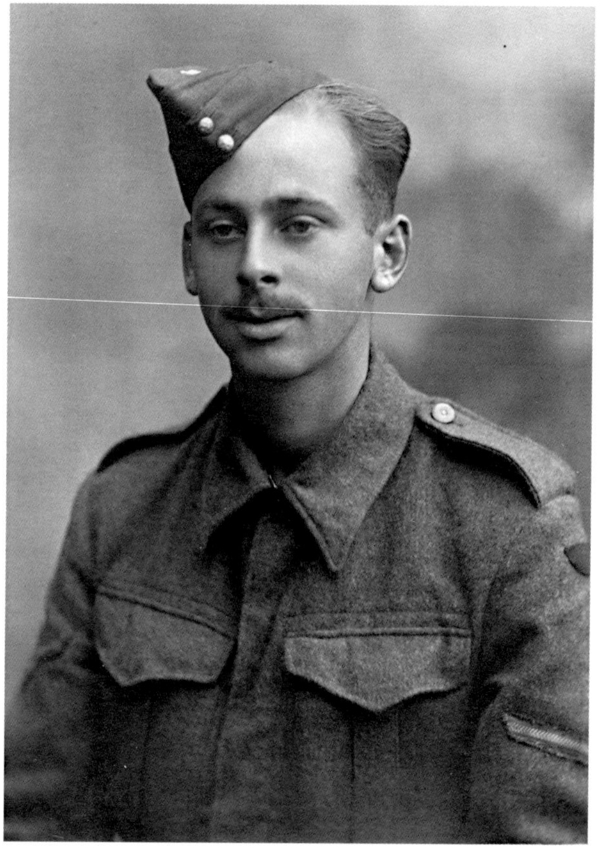

Early days in the DCLI. Jack with first stripe on his way to becoming Sgt. Pender

2 Wartime

A war which was to disrupt the Pender family for six long years. Coming from a fishing family and having spent much of his life "messing about in boats", Jack's brother William (Bill) volunteered for the Royal Navy, while Jack, seeking something more glamorous perhaps, plumped for the RAF hoping to be a fighter pilot. Having since experienced Jack's driving of a car, it must be true to say that if he had made the RAF and became a pilot, then he would either have been a casualty within the average three week-long life of a fighter pilot, or survived as an ace with countless enemy aircraft to his credit. As it happened, as their sister Sylvia, the only child of Nettie and John Pender left at home during the war years, maintains – and I'm sure she's right – it was only because the country's need for soldiers was greater than anything else at the time that both of her brothers were called up for the army, Bill to serve at first with the Somerset Light Infantry and then the Queen's Own Royal West Kent regiment, and Jack with his county regiment, the Duke of Cornwall's Light Infantry.

Joining the regiment's 2nd Battalion, one whose members were "the first of the DCLI to see action in the Second World War and the last to depart from the field of conflict", it was not long before he was in France as part of the British Expeditionary Force (BEF) and about to begin several years of total war service. Although he spoke of his war experiences but rarely, and then often in a humorous vein, few saw as much action as Jack did. Wounded at least twice, and reported "Missing, killed in action" – one can only imagine the anguish this caused his parents – he was caught up in the defeat suffered by the British army in the 1939–40 campaign. While the majority of his battalion, who, "since the start of the German onslaught had been almost continuously engaged in digging, marching and fighting", made their escape via Dunkirk, he was one of those who became separated and had to make his way "walking across France" to Cherbourg. It says everything for his physical strength and strength of mind that, with everything stacked against him, he was able to do just that and so come back safely to this country.

Further active service followed in North Africa, one of the actions being the battle of Medjez-el-Bab prior to the capture of Tunis. Jack was to write a poem "They, Too, Were Young", in tribute to his pals who died in that action the last verse of which carries a message for all mankind:

> And as your life in peace is run,
> And you grow old, remember still
> Those boys who never will,
> Because they died when they were young!"

It was a campaign which ended at Cape Bon in 1943 – and Jack did like telling this story, accompanied by much rubbing of his hands – where "the 2nd DCLI was instrumental in effecting the surrender of the last enemy troops in Africa".By one of those tricks of fate in war, he was actually handed their surrender by the General commanding the thousands of German and Italian troops "who stood by the roadside waiting to give themselves up." Then came the Italian campaign and the battle for Monte Cassino, during which he subsequently discovered that his brother Bill was on one hill while he was on another being bombed and shelled by their enemy on alternate nights. Somehow he survived it all, happily both brothers survived it all – Jack had such a reputation for being lucky when in action, for having a charmed life, that members of his platoon would often ask to be placed with him when trouble was about to start – but then, just when it seemed that the battalion was to be given a well deserved rest it was sent instead to Greece.

As the history of the DCLI records, “There it found itself taking part in a very different sort of conflict in which there was often no visible enemy, but one in which danger lurked around every street corner. The battalion had to adapt itself quickly to a modus operandi which has since become familiar to every soldier, one which involved the doctrine of “hearts and minds”. Even when the European War was over the battalion was still engaged in counter-terrorist operations in the Greek hinterland.” Jack’s luck held out, however, and while awaiting his return to this country, he was able to return to sanity and to resume his art studies at the Athens School of Art. As he often said later, “This was the best thing that happened to me during the war.”

But it was not the only thing, while in Greece he met a young lady he liked so much she came close to becoming his wife. On a lighter note, there was also the brief encounter he had with a Harley Davidson motor bike he found in a ditch. For the first time in the war, as an infantryman, he had “wheels” and he made the very most of them until, that is, the day he met a group of GIs who promptly confiscated his precious bike. As he said, “Couldn’t argue, there were too many of them!”.

In his memoir of his grandfather Will George, he tells of his return to “Civvy Street”. Quite by chance, “or some intricate design”, he and his brother Bill came home to their parents and their sister Sylvia, almost at the same time. “I arrived a few days after my brother. My grandfather was not in his chair and my questioning brought the news that he was very ill in bed. As I rushed the stairs my mother tried to stop me. “Have your food first, you’ll be upset, he’s not as you remember.” But I stood by his bed, his wasted face covered with wisps of white hair. “Look, father, see who’s here’” my mother whispered. The eyes flickered open, there was a radiance, his hand groped and found mine. To my mother he said, “You should be the happiest woman, I’m the happiest man.” The next day he died.”

While Jack always admired his grandfather for having the determination to survive until “the boys” came home from the war, he showed much the same determination himself some 53 years later in surviving until his son Jason’s wedding. Ever optimistic, not long before he died Jack spoke of a dream he had had in which he was 106 years old!

Memories of his war years were revived for him when, in 1998, he came together once again with Jeremy le Grice to share a show in the Rainyday Gallery, Penzance – they had shared one there in the previous year when they exhibited 50 paintings to celebrated the gallery's 50th exhibition since opening. An exhibition which was to be Jack's last picture show, it was a particularly poignant occasion as the link between this "unconquerable when united" pair of painters was forged, albeit unknowingly at the time, during the BEF's retreat from France. While 22 years old Private Jack Pender, who was twice asked to take a commission, on his first and last day with the DCLI, was fighting and "stanking" his way towards Cherbourg and eventual return to this country, such are the fortunes of war that 27 years old Lt. Andrew Le Grice, father of Jeremy, was killed during the final withdrawal at Dunkirk.

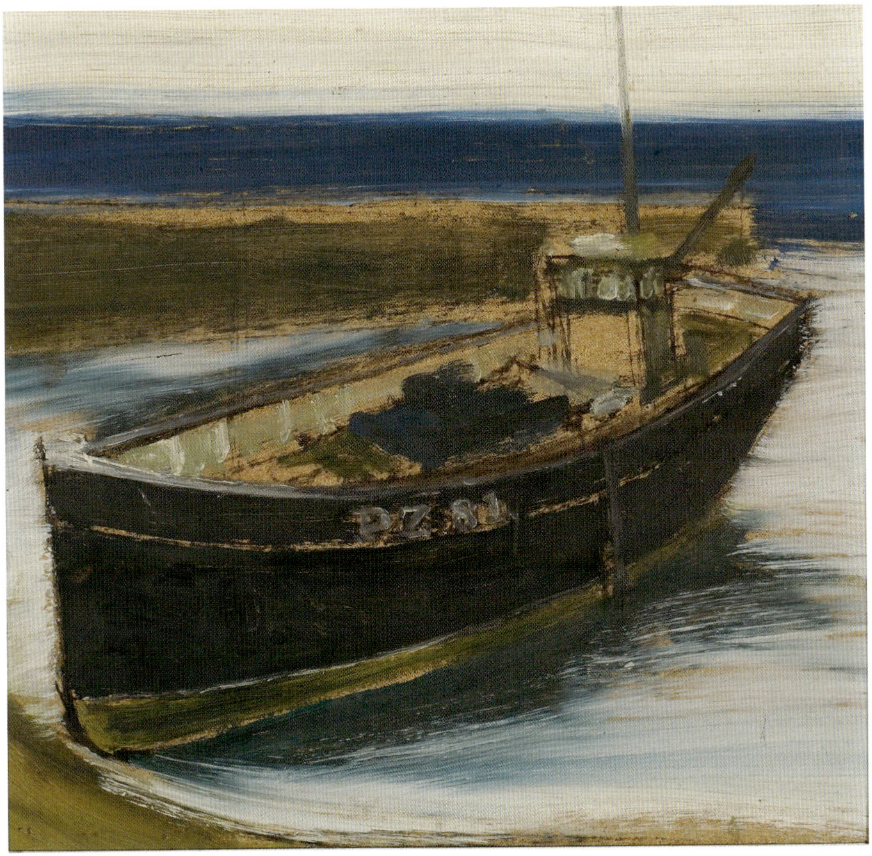

Study for painting Lyonesse, 1950, oil on board. See p32

2 Peace

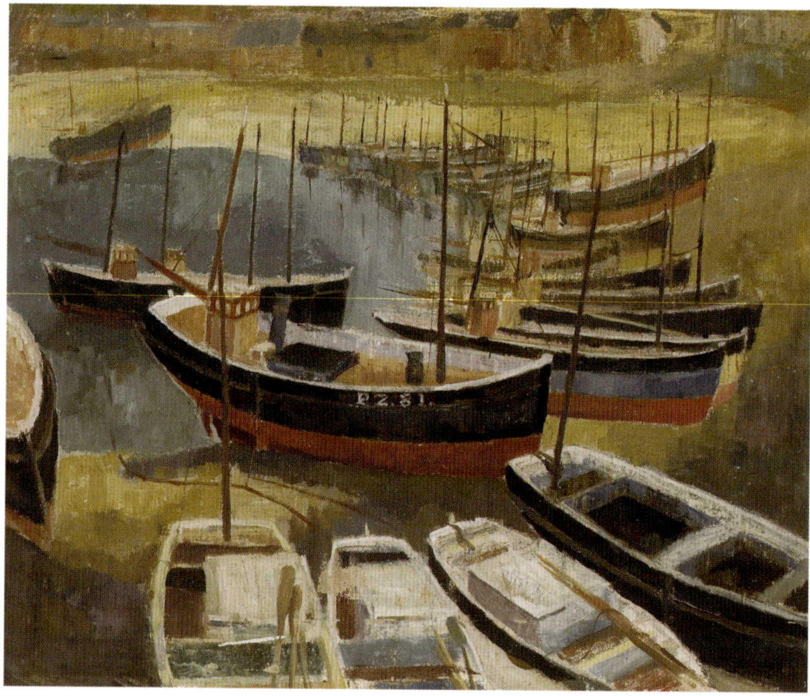

Boats, c1940's, oil on canvas

While his experience of six long years of total war, must have changed him to some degree, just how it affected him is not known. Jack probably didn't even think about it. After all, it was years before such words and phrases as counselling and post traumatic stress came into being, but a time when the thousands of servicemen returning to civilian life were left to adjust, "to get on with it", as best they could. In that respect Jack was luckier than many in that he had his interrupted art studies to pursue and, although it meant leaving his beloved Mousehole again, it was not long before he was busy picking up and repairing the broken threads of his fractured art career.

He attended Exeter School of Art and the West of England School of Art in Bristol, where he gained his A.T.D. (Art Teacher's Diploma) and, while it has been said that at the former establishment he studied under John Skeaping and Clifford Fishwick, and at the latter under Paul Feiler and Claude Rogers, he was not "under" any of them. Neither a beginner nor a raw recruit, with stints at Penzance and Athens Schools of Art beneath his belt, a mature student in every sense, he was very much the equal of each of the four, his connection with them being a collaboration, with Jack giving them as much as they gavc him. He went on, in fact, to become firm friends with Clifford Fishwick, later Principal of Exeter School of Art who, when he began exhibiting his own work, was quick to acknowledge the influence Jack had had upon it and the debt he owed to him.

On completion of his studies Jack set out on what was to be a long career with education in art, teaching first of all at Plymouth Technical School, and then at Britannia, Royal Naval College, Dartmouth. While he was happy at both places, it was his stay at the latter he enjoyed the more. There he was not only given the officer status he had denied himself when an infantryman and, of course, granted access to the wardroom, but, above all else, was also encouraged to practise his own painting.

Dartmouth, Assembly of Sail Training Ships for the Tall Ships' Race, Torbay to Lisbon, June 1956, oil on board

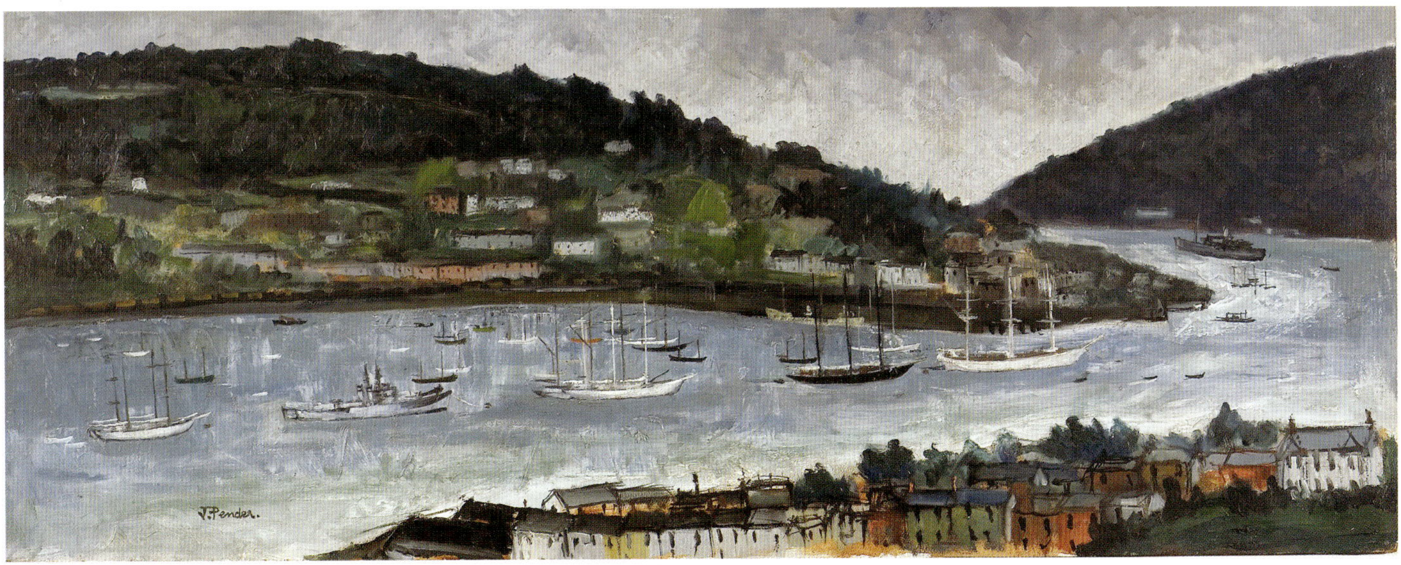

3 Return to Mousehole

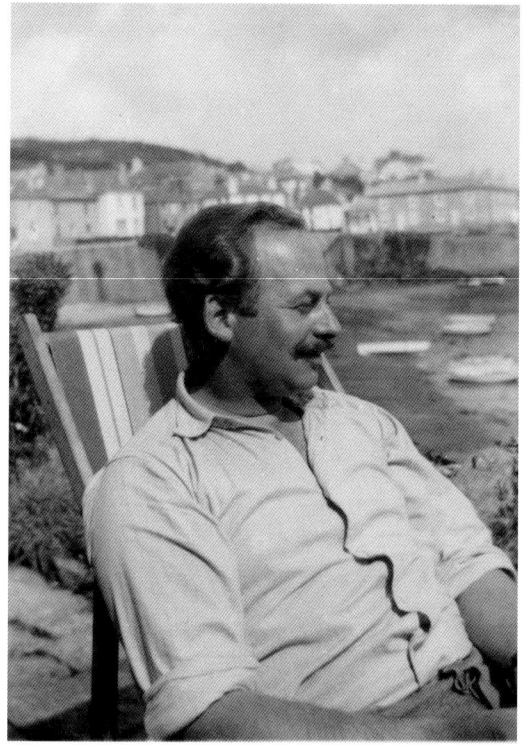

Jack on the terrace of his cottage, viewing what he called 'the Promised Land'. Mousehole late 1950's

However, as seductive as his working conditions were, they were on the wrong side of the Tamar and after a while the call of Cornwall, particularly that of his home port of Mousehole became too alluring to resist and, in 1956, Jack ("PZ 81") came back to where he "belonged". As he said at the time, "This was where I was born. I had to return to work, to teach and to paint."

An important move in more ways than one, it led to his marriage two years later to Madeleine, a talented artist in her own right, and a lady whom he had first met when she was but one year old. Although born in Essex, Madeleine had been coming to Mousehole regularly for years as her family roots were in the village. As it happened, Jack and Madeleine were distant cousins, and shared a common ancestry dating back to the 1780's. Jack subsequently became the proud father of their three children – Robin, now a solicitor, Jason, now a graphic designer, and Tamsin, now an artist. I use the word "proud" advisedly in describing Jack as a father as no one was more proud of his children than he was. Ever ready to expound upon their achievements, it was the only time he ever came close to being a bore and had to be reminded that he was not the only father in the world and that other people had children. To be fair to him, Jack took such telling in good part, although it never stopped him and he continued to voice his pride in his children until the very end.

Now, as his children say, the tables have been turned, and they are as proud of him as he was of them. Jack encouraged them to criticise his work which they did willingly as they favoured most of what he was doing. What Jack failed to appreciate, however, was how difficult it was for them being the son or daughter of such a well-known artist in such a small village and having on occasion to defend his semi-abstract paintings, and the fact that it seemed as if he couldn't draw "a proper boat". Despite all, they remained loyal, admired their father's character, conviction and commitment to his art, his strength of will and refusal to follow fashion, ultimately coming to recognise and realise that, in considering the combination of their great-grandfather W.J. "Will" George and their father Jack, they proudly stand "on giant shoulders".

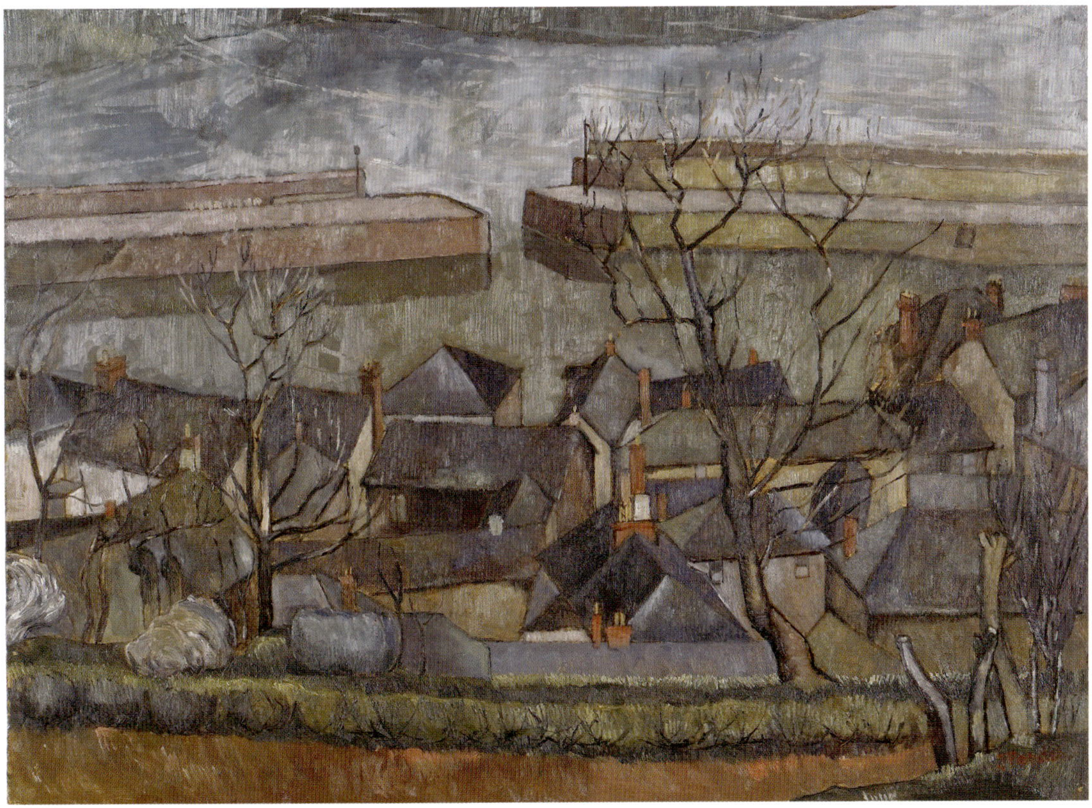

Mousehole from Love Lane, c1950's, oil on board

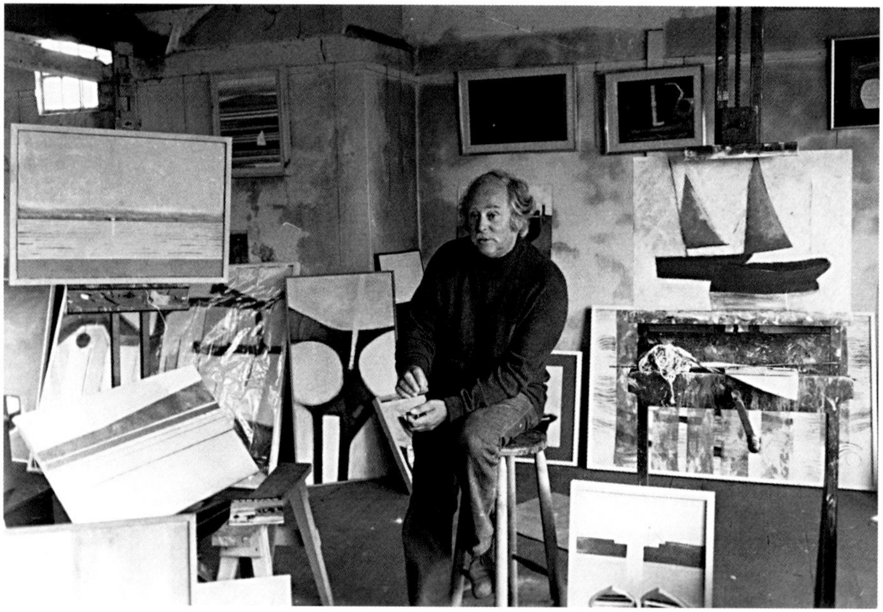

1975, Jack in his beloved Mousehole studio which he had to vacate shortly afterwards

Worth noting at this stage in Jack's career how the advent of his children affected his painting with his boats becoming noticeably fatter and fuller. One of them, painted in 1959, and exhibited at the Belgrave Gallery, London for instance, in a solo show spanning 30 years of his career, actually carried the title of "Pregnant Punt".

Fond of other children as well as his own, Jack once jumped into the harbour at Mousehole and saved a boy from drowning --a brave deed he never elaborated upon but simply shrugged off as being all in a day's work, something anyone else would done if they had been there – he taught generations of children at Treswithian Secondary Modern School, later Camborne Comprehensive School. An excellent, if unorthodox, teacher, as the head of the school's large Art and Design department, he was, if anything, ahead of his time. One of the first to take advantage of the Cornwall Education Committee's collection of works of art set up in 1963, and also one of the first to contribute to it with his "Boats in the Gap", painted in 1961, he lined the school's corridors with paintings by fellow artists such as Terry Frost and Patrick Heron, and also found the ways and means of getting such practising artists as Breon O'Casey and Donald Swan on the staff as part-time visitng artists. A great encourager, he not only got the very best out of his pupils but also from the staff in his large department, allowing them to develop their own ideas and methods of teaching.

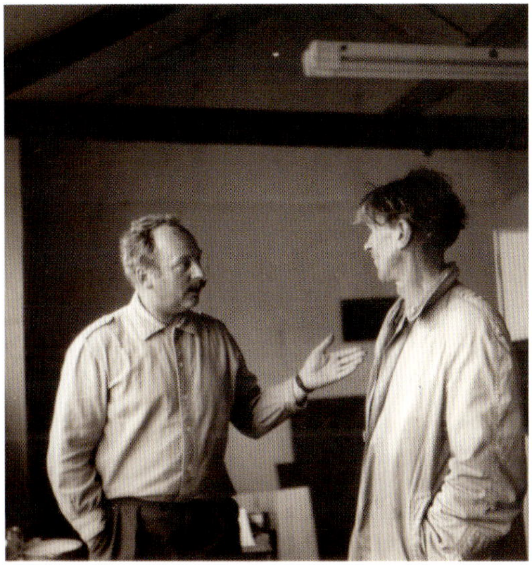

Jack in conversation with fellow painter Johnny Wells. Possibly Jack's studio early 1960's

Along the way he was also to influence me. Among other things he was to teach me, what he called, the gentle art of teaching by remote control. An art form frowned upon by the powers to be, but one which worked; it typified Jack's style and approach to teaching. He possessed such flair, energy and enterprise, no classroom could contain him and the capers he was involved in within the school were legion. Perhaps the most memorable was his painting of one of the school's caretaking staff. Jack kept promising, or threatening, to paint him one day, and that is just what he did. Somehow he talked his unsuspecting victim into standing in front of his class, dressed him in overalls, and then proceeded not to paint his portrait but to, quite literally, paint him from head to toe. I remember Jack sending a message for me to come down to his art room and see his latest painting. Rubbing his hands together and smiling all over his face, he said, "How about this for a piece of living art then, boy." The surprising outcome of it all was the delight with which his subject accepted the happening. He was honoured, not to say thrilled, and for ages afterwards went around the school boasting of how he had been painted by Mr. Pender.

Teaching at the same school and coming from the same part of the world led to me sharing a car with Jack for a number of years. I've already hinted at his fondness for speed and, while he could handle it and was a good driver, he was also often an angry one. The inventor of road rage, he could not stand anyone on the road doing anything which, in his eyes, was wrong. The danger lay in the fact that he often wanted to correct the mistakes of other drivers. The most memorable in this respect occurred in the centre of Penzance when the driver of a bus did something which annoyed Jack. He slammed on his brakes, leapt from the car, ran across the road and hammered

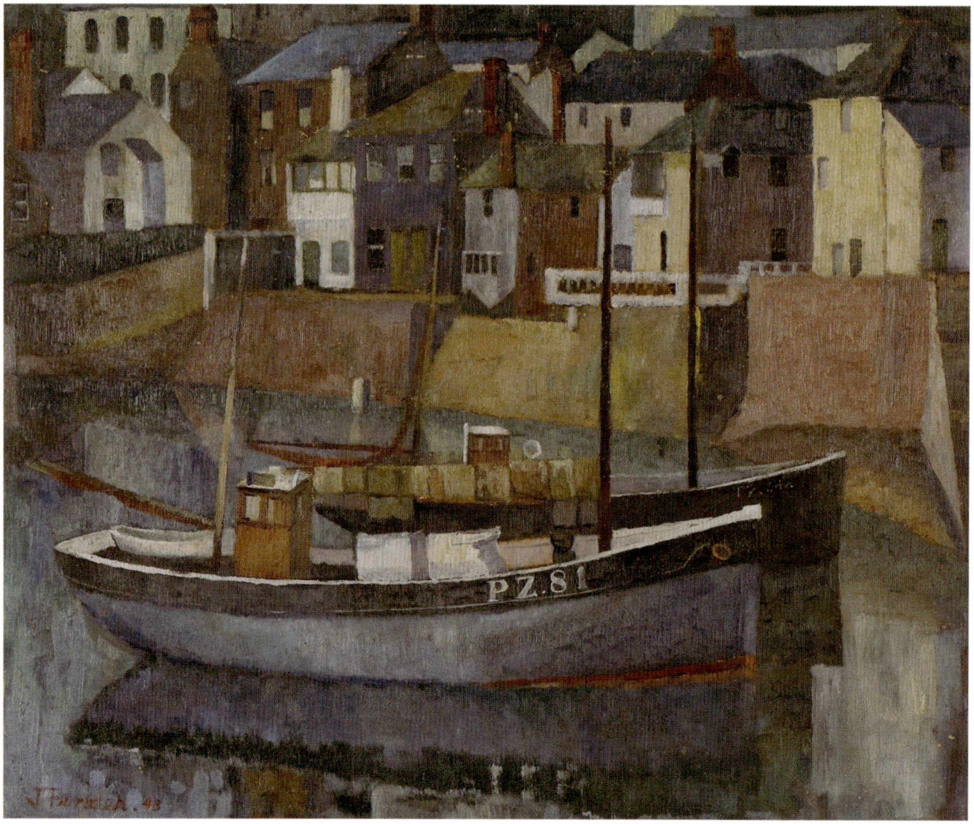
Untitled, 1948, oil on board

on the bus driver's door, shouting and shaking his fist at the driver who, amazed, looked at Jack as if he was mad. Then, ignoring the traffic which had built up while all this was happening, Jack returned to the car and far from being in a rage, turned, grinned at me, rubbed his hands together, and said, "He won't forget that in a hurry, boy. His first meeting with a true knight of the road!"

Jack's ability to switch on and off in that way was but one of his many charms. Another was his generosity. An artist who would rather give away than sell a painting, it was through his willingness to take me with him when on his trips to St. Ives, often when on our way home from school and he had a painting to hand in at the Penwith Gallery, that I came to know so many other artists. Jack was my passport to the town's post-war avant garde art scene, and I've always been grateful to him for being instrumental in opening so many studio doors for me, from that of Wilhelmina Barns-Graham's to Tony O'Malley's.

Then, too, when I was about to have my first book of poems published, I asked Jack if he would illustrate it for me, whereupon he not only did so "per gratis", but when the book appeared gave me his original drawings as a souvenir of the occasion. Among the poems in that collection,

"Penwith Poems", was one which I wrote after a visit to Jack's studio at his request to "come and see my latest, boy, like to know what you think of it." A seminal work if ever there was one, it knocked me over, and my recovery resulted in this poem which I include here not as a trumpet-blowing exercise for myself but because Jack liked and appreciated it so much. As he said when he first read it, "Not bad for a Bucca, boy."

Untitled, c1970's, lithograph

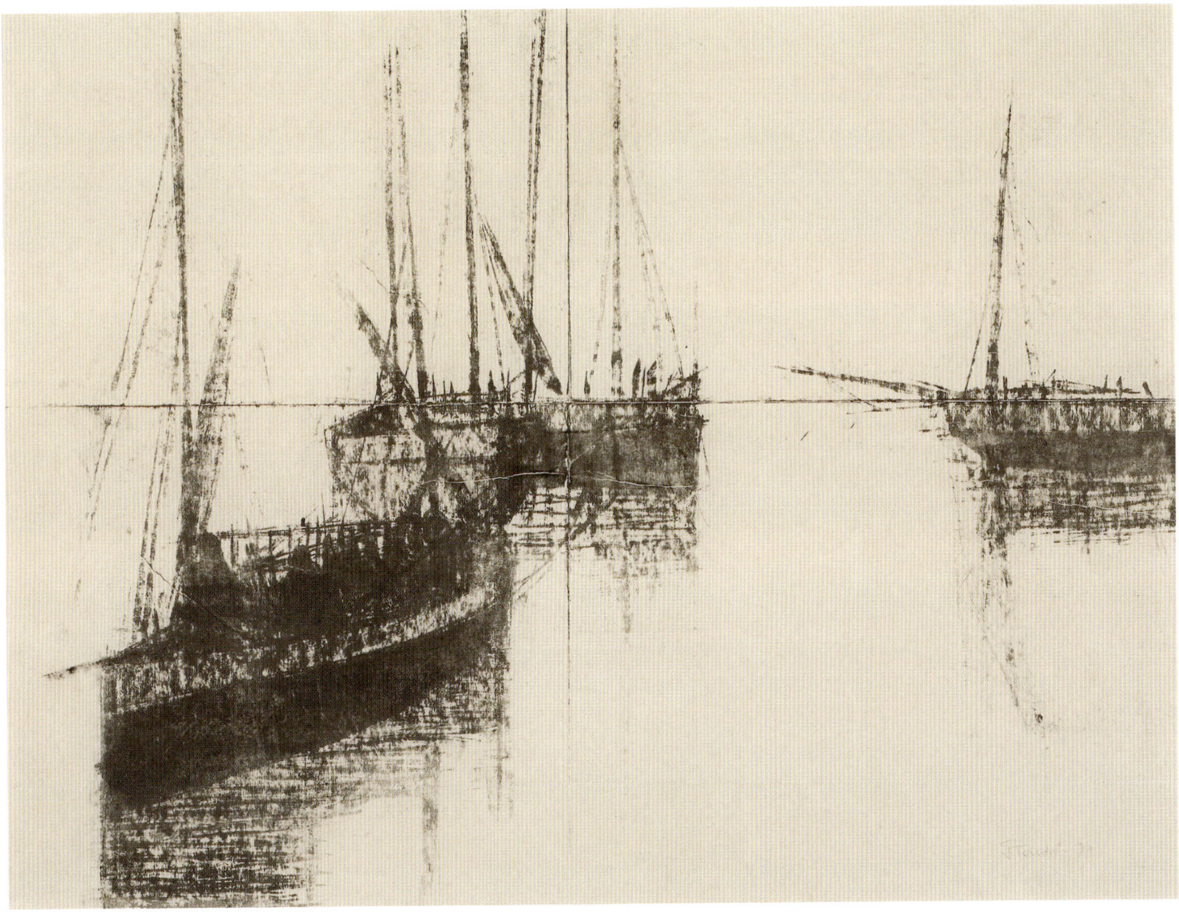

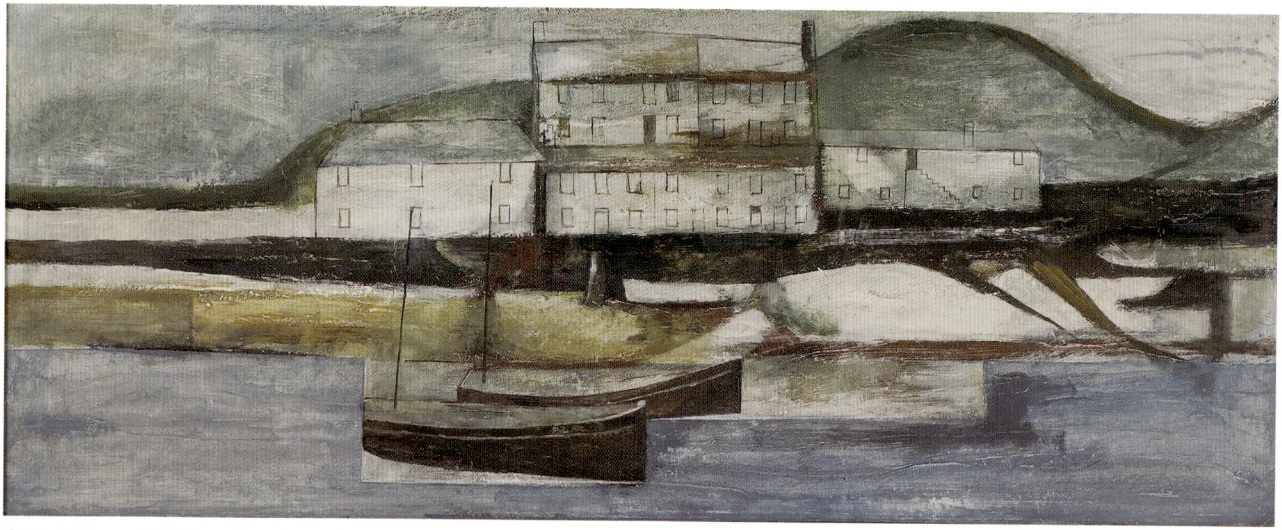

Seas Edge, c1960's, oil on board

SISTER BOATS
(on a painting by Jack Pender)

Black-bottomed and broad in the beam
they strain at the frame
that timidly holds them.

Spinsters of this parish
filled to their gunnels with pride
bulging they boast
of the catches that could have been theirs,
of the mackerel and men
who drift in their dreams,
each doing her best
to better the other.

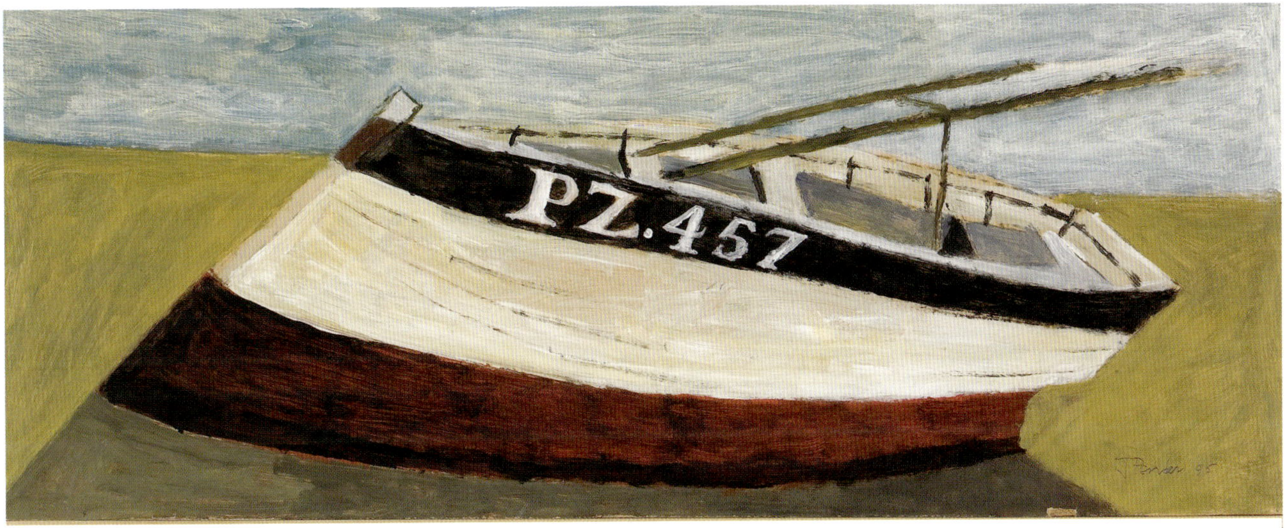

The Bass Boat, 1995, acrylic on board

Moored to a white wall
starry-eyed they gaze
at the schoolroom
where chapel children
once came and chanted
for those in peril
– Methodist Hymn Book, Number 917 –

Their varnished smiles
spread from stem to stern
covering the cracks
as they smugly recall
the prizes for solid Sunday attendance,
the anniversary anthems,
the signing of the pledge.

Prim and proper they paddled

the spring tides of youth.
Tee-totalled, tight-thighed and sou'westered
– no drop inside or out –
they lowered the boom
on Tom Bawcock's boys and their beer,
closed the gap
against the run of the wild sou'easters.

Weather-bound in their bible-bound cottage
they listened to the pilchard-driven screams
of the netted and the hooked.
Not for us, and Amen,
they said to themselves,
and now,
as their sea legs warp
yearning to open
and salt tears spring from seams
that want caulking
they strain at the painter
that keeps them there
frightening the frame
that timidly holds them.

Untitled, 1991, acrylic on board

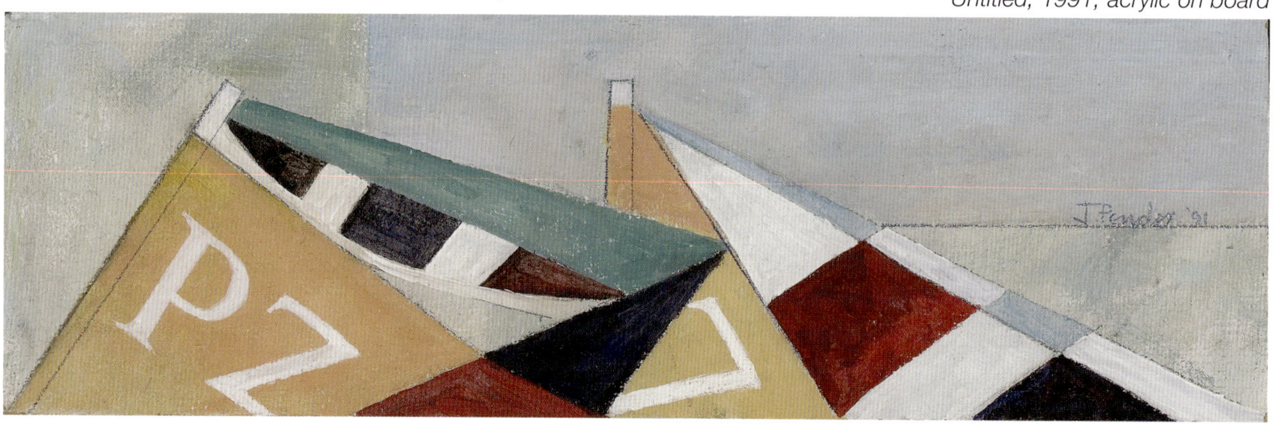

3 And later

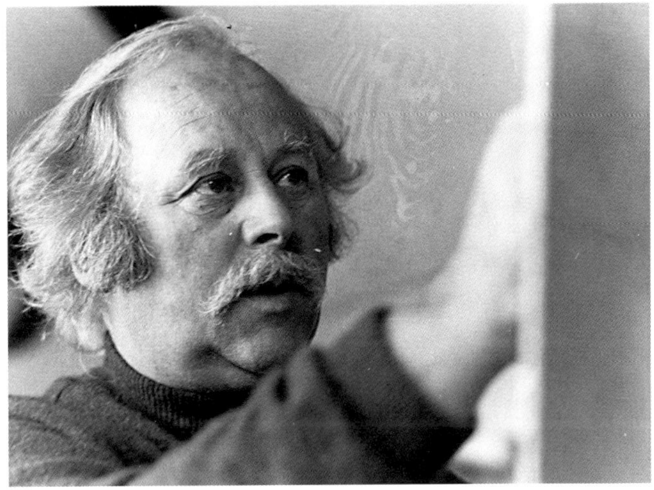

Jack in the 1970's, at his best, and happiest, when painting

Larger than life, as complex as he was colourful, while in his heyday with his cravat, moustache and smile, Jack resembled Frans Hals' "The Laughing Cavalier" at the same time he could be curiously shy and modest. It is no exaggeration to say that, at the height of his powers and for most people, he "WAS" Mousehole. As much a part of the fabric of the village as the legendary Tom Bawcock, there were months when the BBC seemed to be camped permanently on his doorstep and, among other television programmes he was selected by Angela Rippon for her "Choices" series and for BBC 2's series "Look Stranger". Such media attention suited Jack, convivial to say the least, he was never happier than when he was having a drink, a laugh, or telling a story. Unfortunately, his fondness for "La dolce vita" led to the break up of his family life in the late 1970's, to a divorce after twenty years of marriage at a time when he also lost his studio and caused him to give a solo show he had at the Newlyn Orion Gallery the quite literal title of "On My Knees".

But, against all odds and being a fighter in more ways than one, a champion boxer during his army days, he survived such setbacks, plus a later period of serious ill health – when he wondered if he would ever paint again – to carry on doing so. A member of the Newlyn, Penwith and Plymouth Societies of Artists, he exhibited widely in this country and abroad. There was a time in the 1960's and 70's when I was one the many "groupies" who attended his shows in Cornwall from St. Ives to Sheviock. One of the few Cornish-born artists in the prestigious 1985 St. Ives at the Tate exhibition, although often asked why he did not paint "proper boats" he not

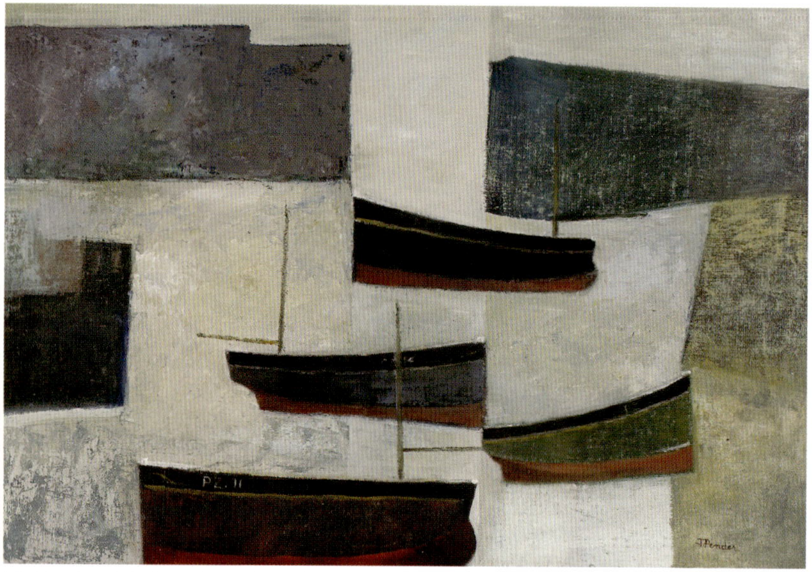

Untitled, c1960's, oil on board

only made the "Pender boat" his own. but influenced a great many other artists as well. An artist who painted straight from the shoulder and who, as he did when boxing in the army, never pulled any punches, often the unseen was more important than the seen in his compositions, he eschewed security and took risks to come up with paintings that, like the man himself, were as honest as the day is long.

Fond of sailing he once had the pleasure of helping to crew the lugger "Barnabas" from Newlyn to Falmouth when he said, "She sails like a witch" a comment which underlined the relationship between man and boat, for Jack, in turn, painted like a wizard,

An accomplished cricketer, he played for the local Artists' XI, and a member of the MCC, as well as an artist, teacher, boxer, soldier and sailor, Jack was also devoted to the place in which he was born and bred. A harbour commissioner for many years and chairman of Mousehole Harbour Authority, he was closely involved in the aftermath of the awful events of December 19, 1981, when the whole crew of the Penlee lifeboat "Solomon Browne", and those they had set out to rescue on that wild night, were lost at sea. He knew every member of that crew, and the disaster affected him deeply. Only days prior to it I had been with him and John Blewett, the lifeboat's emergency mechanic, when, for most of the evening, they pulled my leg about how much better Mousehole's Christmas lights were than those of Newlyn. A trustee of the Penlee lifeboat disaster fund, as an expression of the trustees' gratitude to Lord Goodman for the help he had given them in administering the fund, Jack's painting of the "Solomon Browne" was presented to him in the House of Lords. Again it was typical of Jack's generosity that, when asked to make the painting, he only agreed on the understanding that he would do so for free.

As Cornish as pasties and pilchards and fiercely proud of being so, it is only right and proper that Jack should be remembered in granite: with a polished granite, public seat, installed not far from where he was born and bred by Mousehole's harbour commissioners, which carries the inscription "Millennium 2000, In Memory Of Jack Pender. A Man Of Mousehole.", and by a similarly polished, simple but striking granite gravestone in the cemetery at Paul, which reads JACK PENDER. ARTIST. 1st June 1918 --20th June 1998."

Designed by his son Jason, it also carries a cluster of "Pender boats" and, standing before it recently in a place which is often so cold and cheerless but on a day which was as warm and as bright and blue as the sea in so many of Jack's paintings, I reflected upon and reckoned up the extraordinary amount he had achieved in his lifetime, from his boyhood days when he had watched his "Grandpa" W.J.(Will) George making his paintings to those he had made himself and that were to make him one of Cornwall's foremost modern painters.

As a Newlyn Bucca, I had to admit (while rubbing my hands together), not bad for a Mousehole Cut-throat!

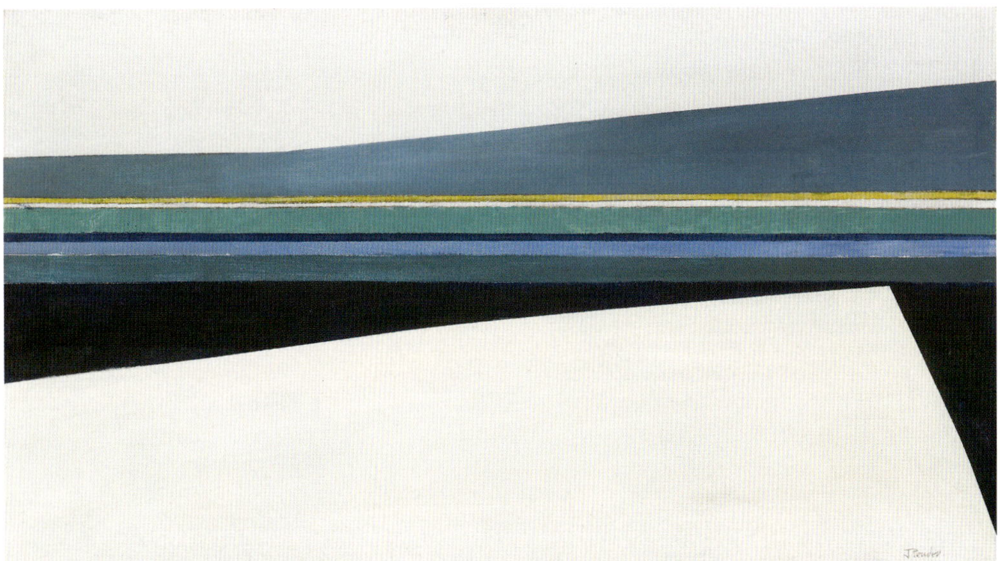

Across the Bay, 1976, oil on canvas

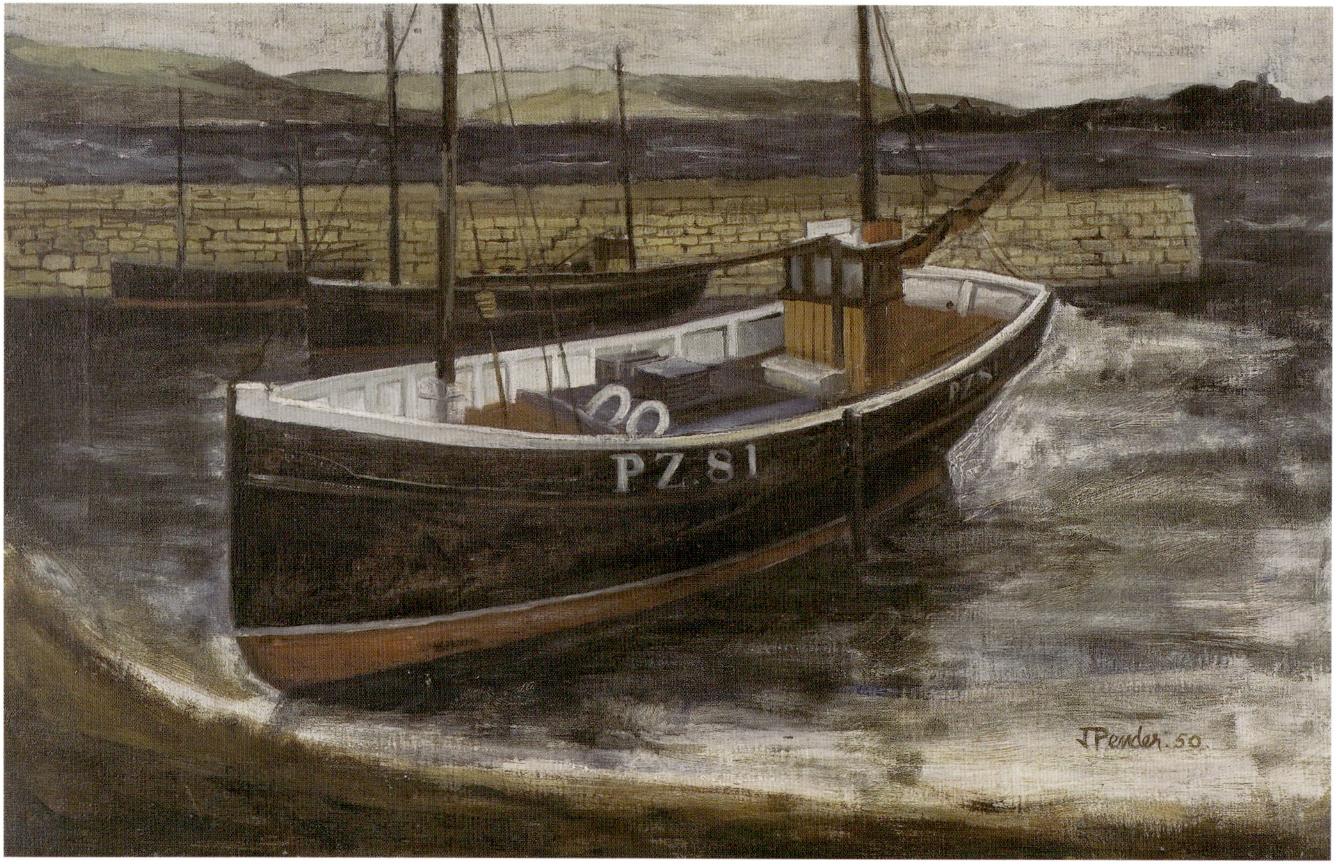

Lyonesse, 1950, oil on canvas

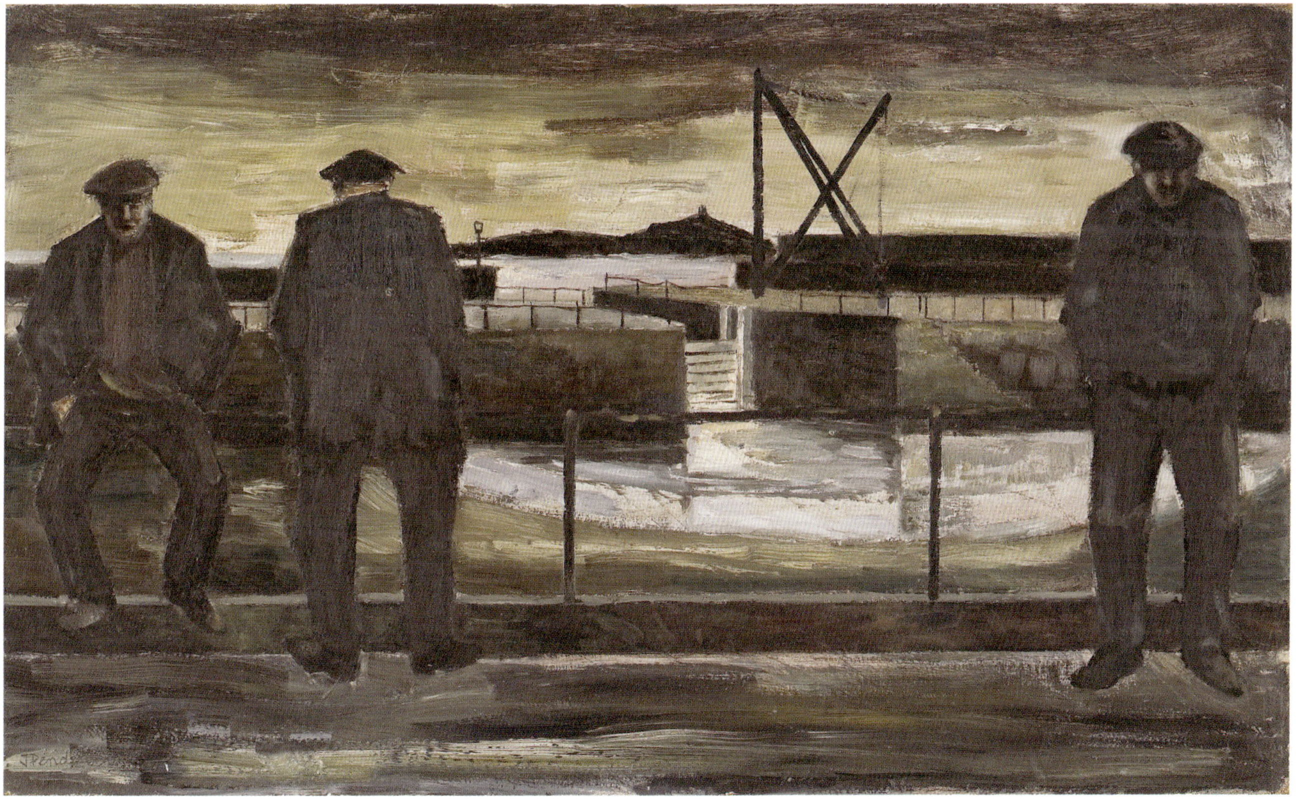

Three Fishermen, c1950's, oil on board

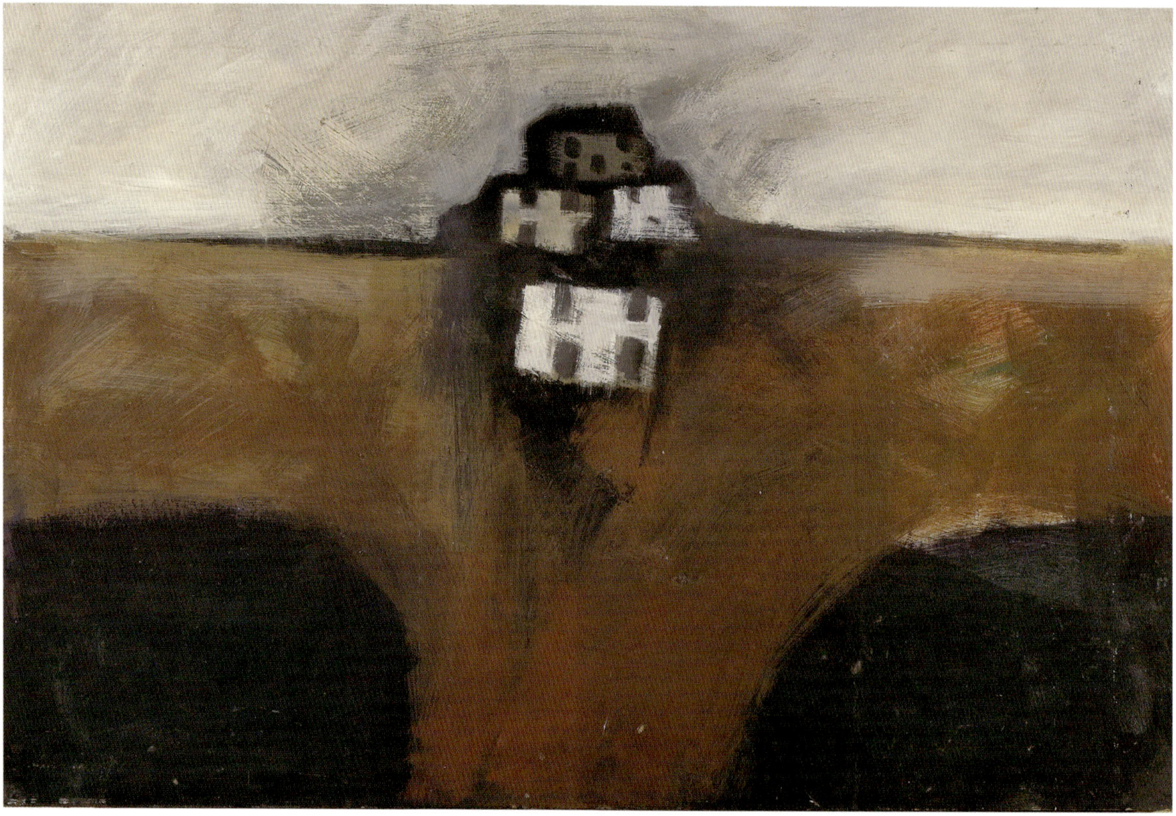

Cottages, 1950's, oil and acrylic on board

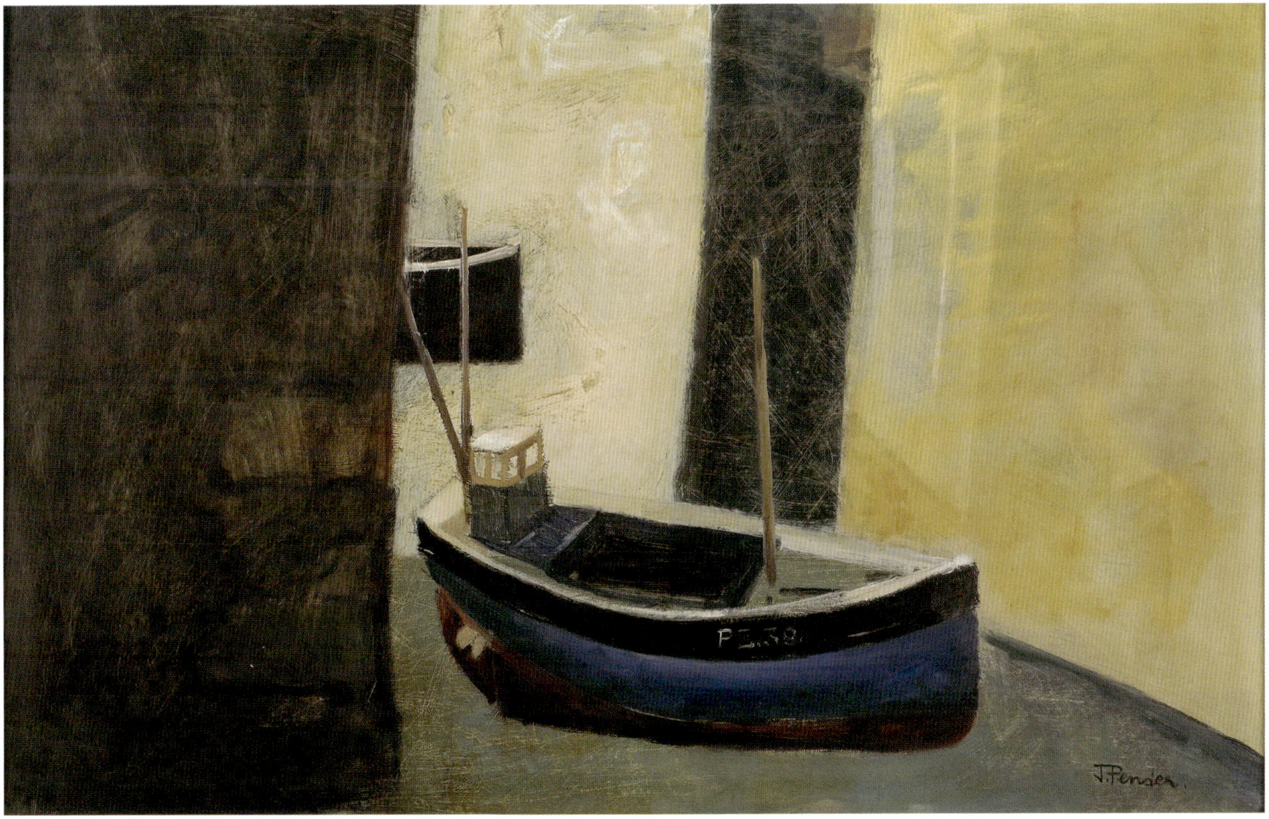

PZ39, undated, oil on board

Mousehole, c1970's, acrylic on board

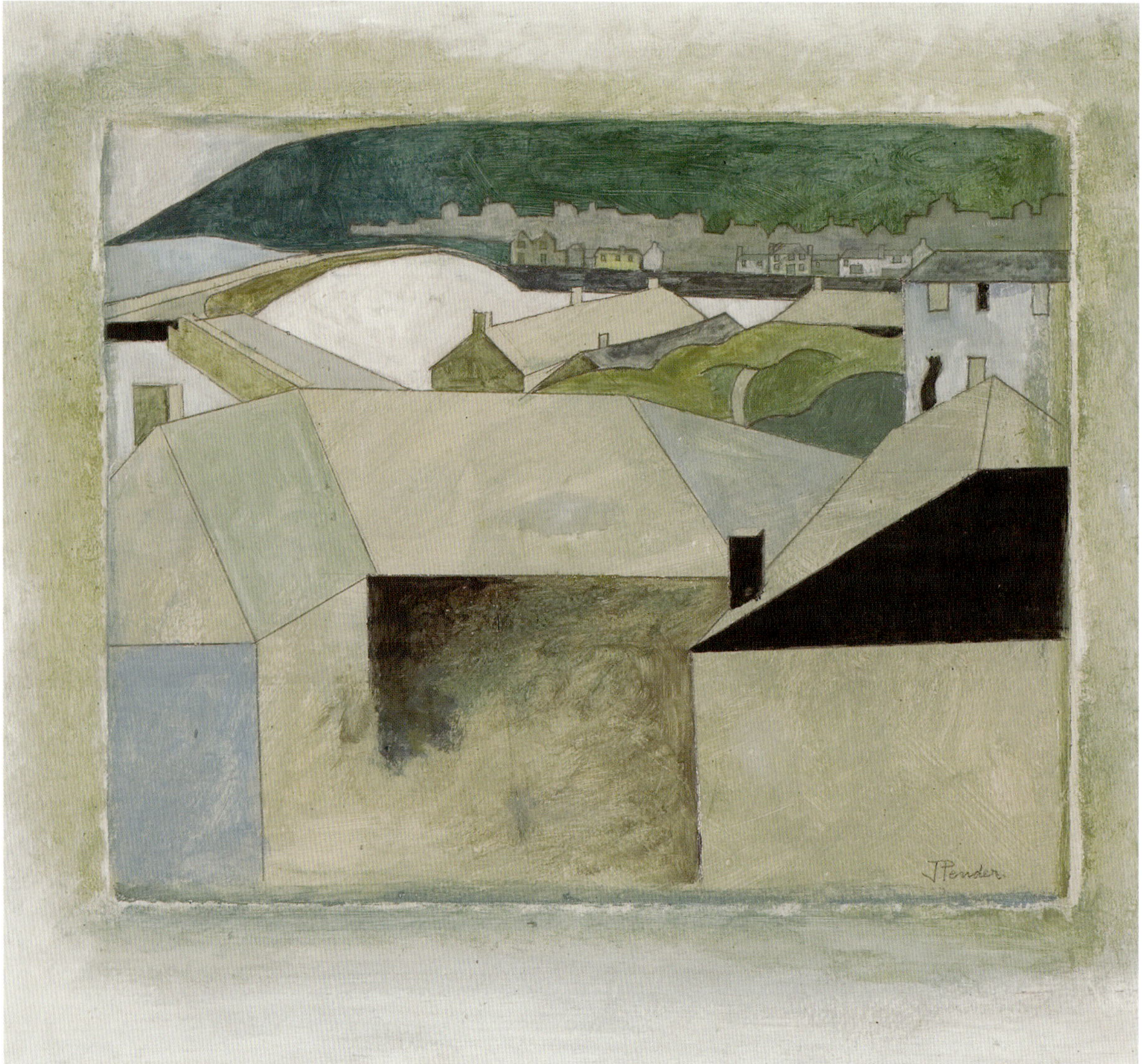

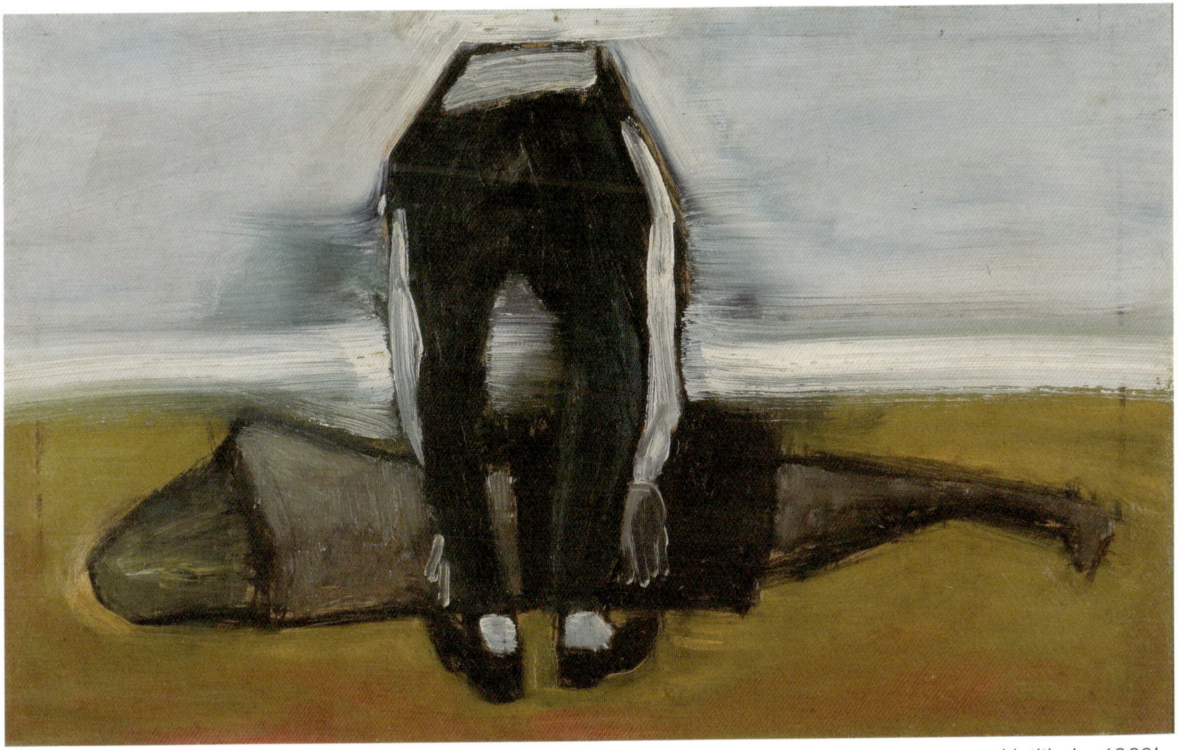

Untitled, c1960's,
oil on board

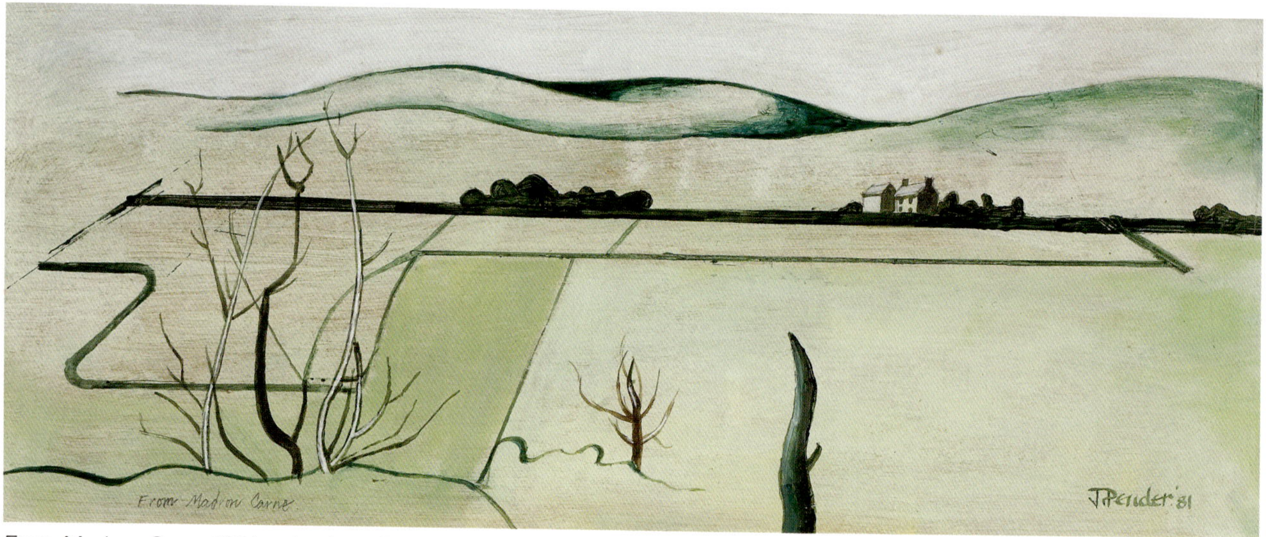

From Madron Carn, 1981, mixed media

Untitled, oil on board

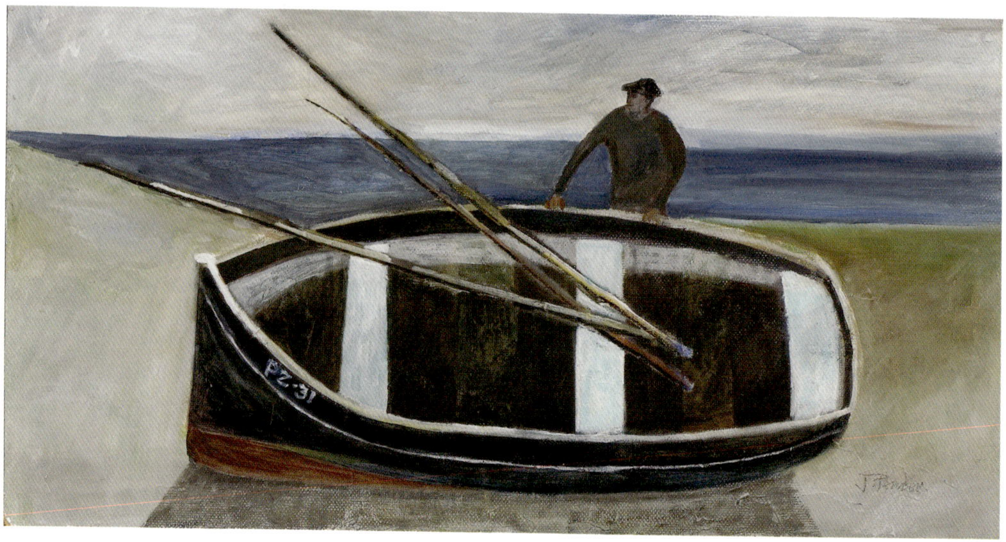

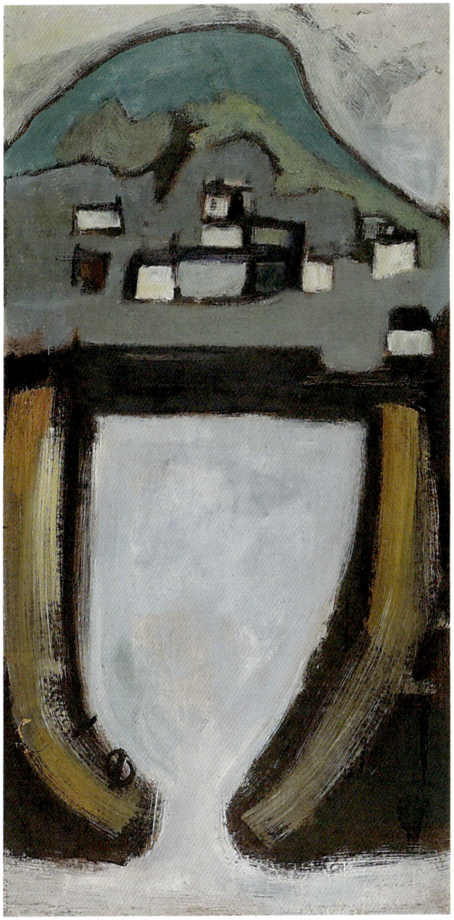
Empty Harbour No2, 1963–72, oil on board

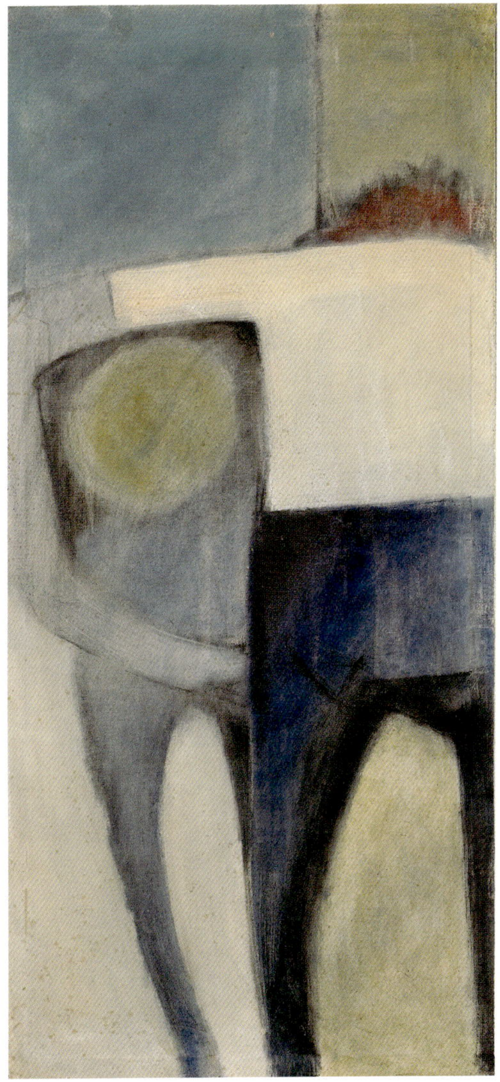
Deposition No4, c1958, oil on canvas

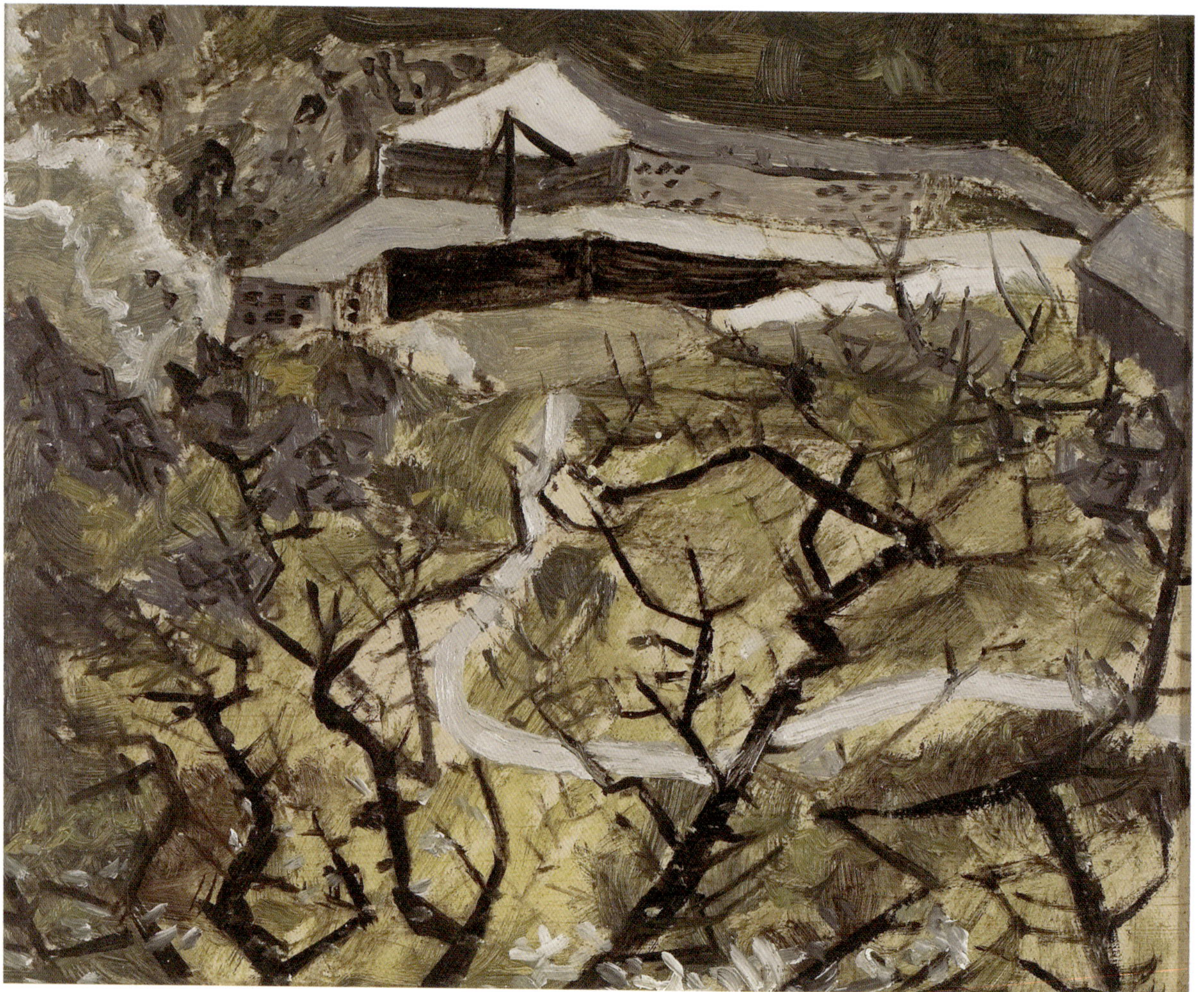

Untitled, c1940's, oil on board

Adrift 2, 1966, oil on board

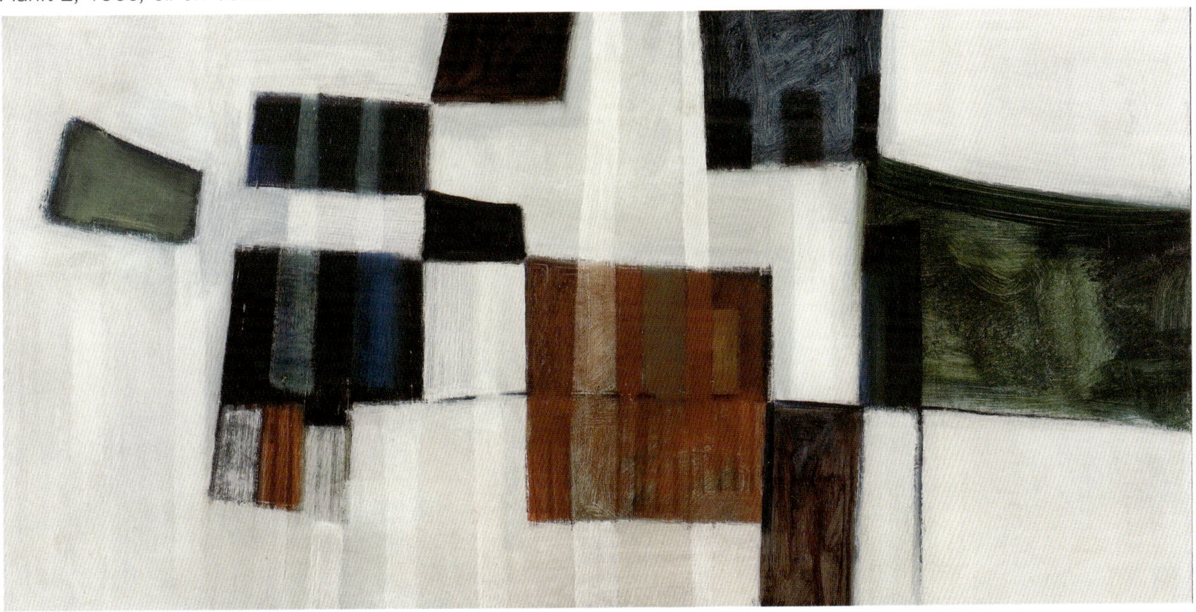

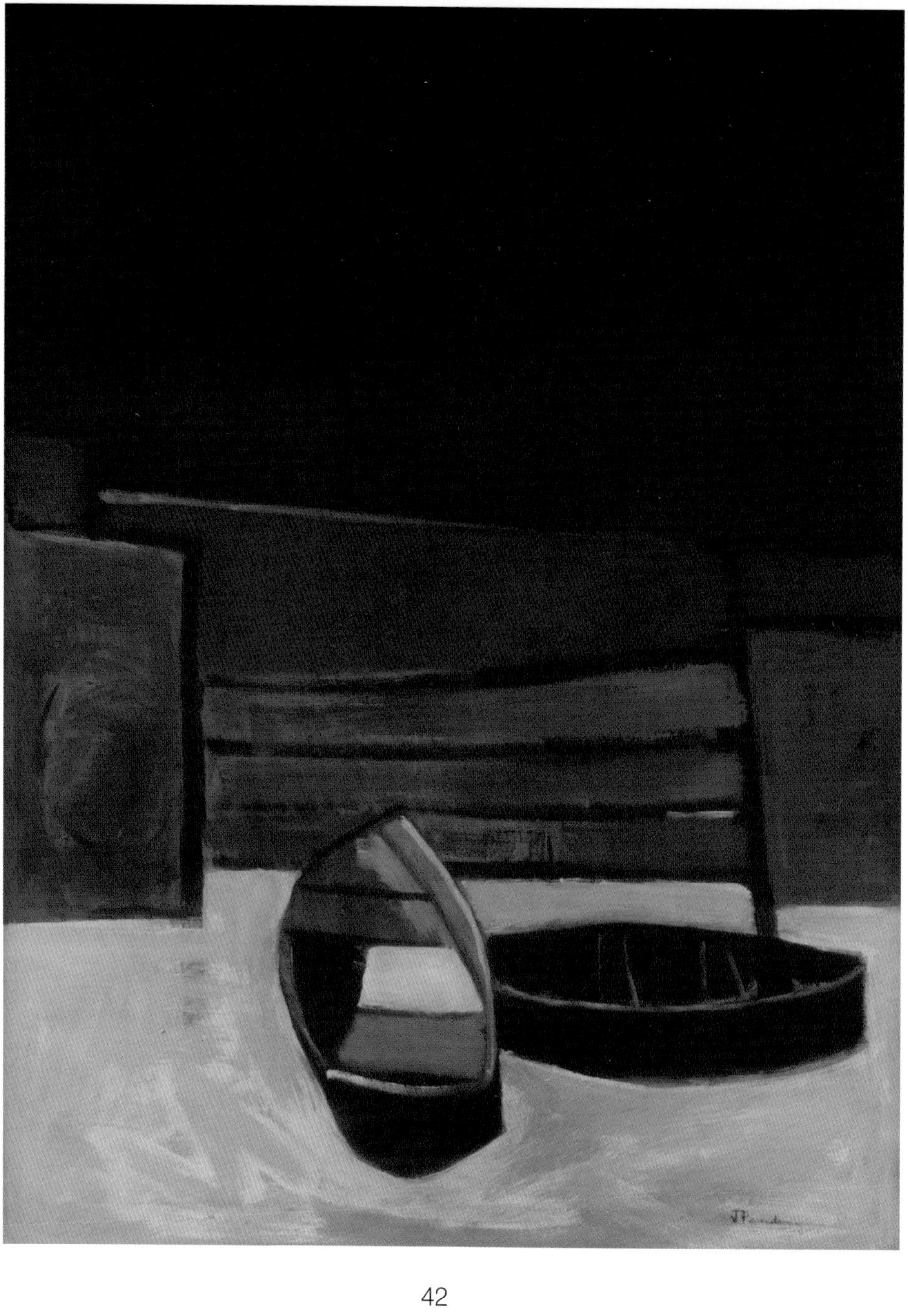

Boats in Baulk No3, 1950, oil on board

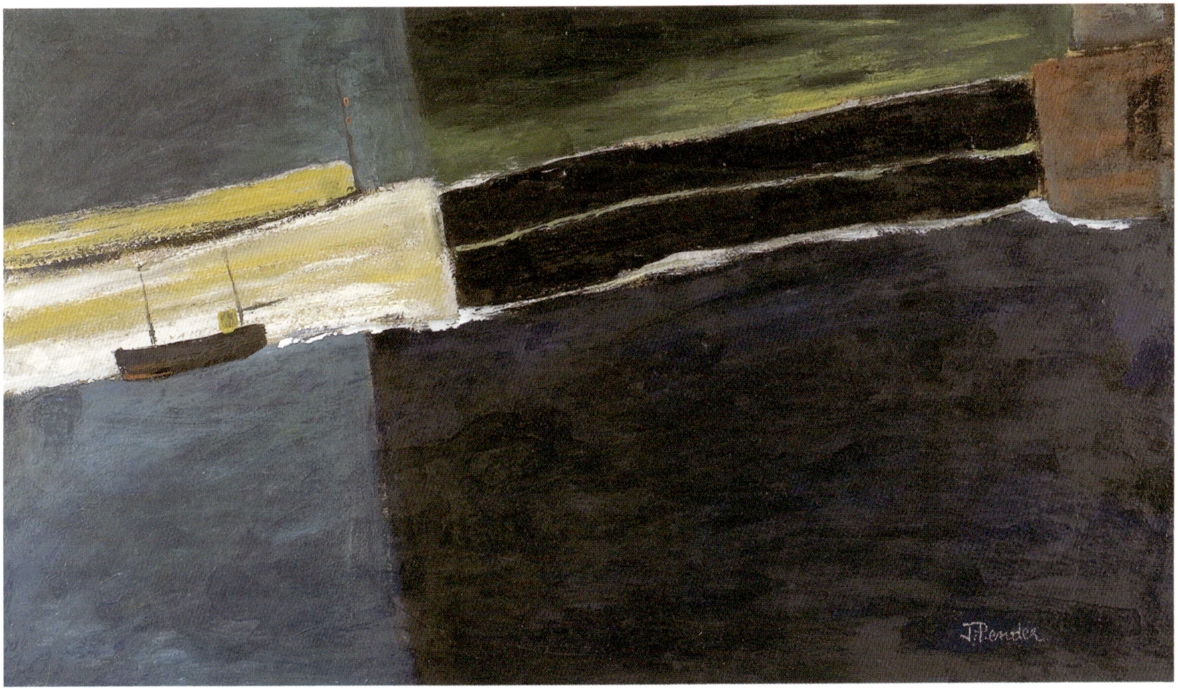

Lyonesse Leaving Harbour, 1981, gouache (painted as a birthday present for Robin Pender 16.09.1981

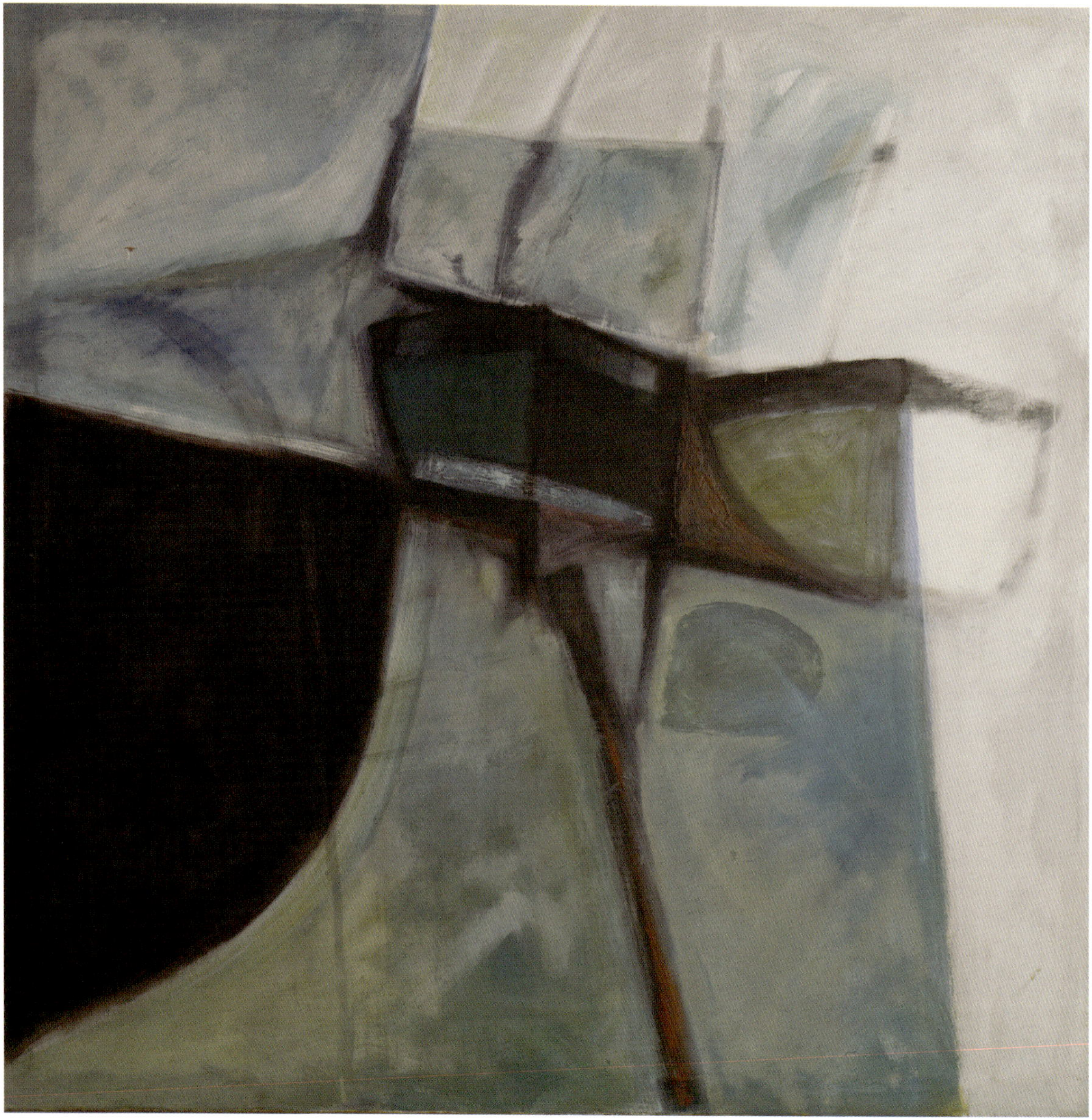

Spring Storm, 1968, oil on canvas

At Moorings, c1970's, oil on hardboard

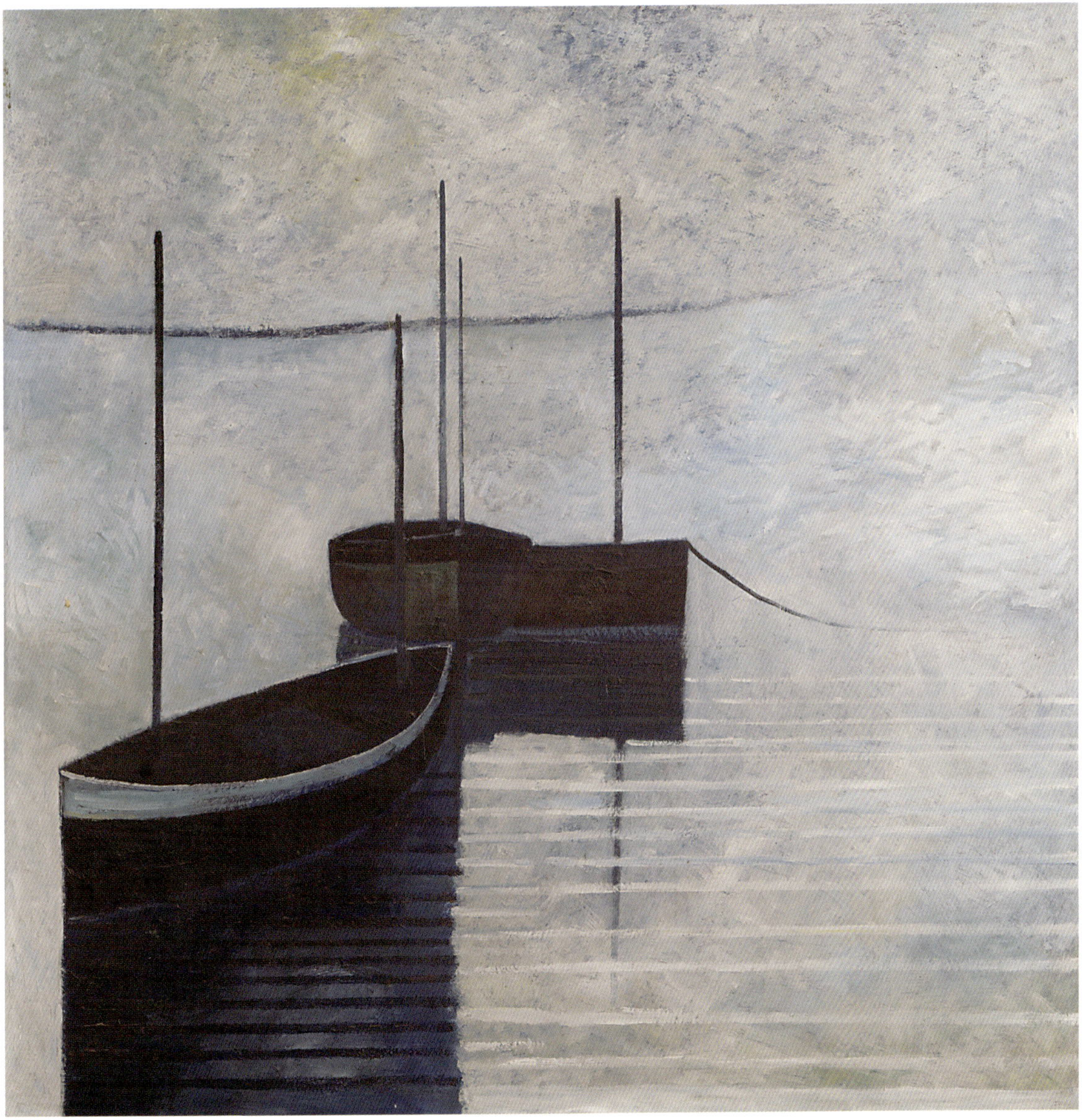

Chronology

1918	Born 1 June in Mousehole, Cornwall
1936	Began painting
1938–39	Attended Penzance School of Art
1939–46	Served with the Duke of Cornwall's Light Infantry
1945–46	Attended Athens School of Art, Greece
1946–49	Attended Exeter School of Art
	Started exhibiting with the Penwith and Newlyn Societies of Artists
1949–50	Attended West of England College of Art, Bristol. Gained his A.T.D.
1950–54	Taught at Plymouth School of Art
1952	Part of Plymouth Society of Artists 9th annual exhibition. Plymouth Art Gallery
1953	Part of Plymouth Society of Artists 10th annual exhibition. Plymouth Art Gallery
1954–56	Taught at Britannia, Royal Naval College, Dartmouth
1954	Elected as a member of the Penwith and the Newlyn Societies of Artists
1956	Came back to live and work in his home port of Mousehole
1958	Married to Madeleine
	Part of the exhibition "Twenty Cornish Painters" Newlyn Art Gallery
1960	Part of the exhibition "Painters in Cornwall" City Art Gallery, Plymouth
1962	Part of the exhibition "West Penwith Painters and Sculptors", Arnolfini Gallery, Bristol
1963	First one-man show, Arnolfini Gallery, Bristol
1964	Part of Belgian exchange exhibition, Feest Palais, Ostend
	Part of four-person show, with Peter Lanyon, Elizabeth and Peter Rainsford, Fore Street Gallery, St. Ives
1967	One-man show. Arnolfini Gallery, Bristol
1968	One-man show. Sheviock Gallery, Torpoint
1972	Part of the exhibition "Artists of Cornwall", University of Birmingham
1973	One-man show. Orion Gallery, Penzance
1974	Elected first chairman of Newlyn Orion Galleries Ltd

	One-man show. Orion Gallery, Penzance
	BBC film. "Artist in a Cornish Harbour"
1976	One-man show. St. Clement's Hall Gallery, Mousehole
	BBC film on Jack Pender in Mousehole
1977	Part of exhibition "Cornwall 1945–55" New Art Centre, London
	One-man show. Exeter University
1978	Loses his studio in Mousehole
	BBC film in Angela Rippon's series "Choice"
1979	One-man show, "On My Knees", Newlyn Orion Gallery
1981	Part of exhibition "Ten Cornish Artists", Cuxhaven, Germany.
	Penlee lifeboat disaster, loss of the "Solomon Browne"
1982	Presentation of his painting "Solomon Browne" to Lord Goodman, House of Lords
	Part of three-man show, "Three Men in a Boat", Chenil Gallery, London
1985	Part of exhibition "St. Ives 1939-64", Tate Gallery, London
	1986-87 Part of travelling exhibition "Celtic Vision", Madrid, Brittany, Dublin, Cardiff and Newlyn
1987,8,9	Part of annual exhibitions "Some of the Moderns", Belgrave Gallery, London
1989	One-man show Leon Suddaby Fine Art, Penzance
1990	Part of "Century of Art in Cornwall 1889–1989" County Museum & Art Gallery, Truro
	One-man show Belgrave Gallery, London
1990	Paintings exhibited in United Nations Building, New York. U.S.A.
1991	One-man show Leon Suddaby Fine Art, Penzance
1996	Part of mixed exhibition, Rainyday Gallery, Penzance
1997	Two-man show with Jeremy Le Grice, Rainyday Gallery, Penzance
1998	Two-man show with Jeremy Le Grice, Rainyday Gallery, Penzance
1998	Died, 20 June aged 80
2008	Exhibition at Penlee House Gallery and Museum, Penzance

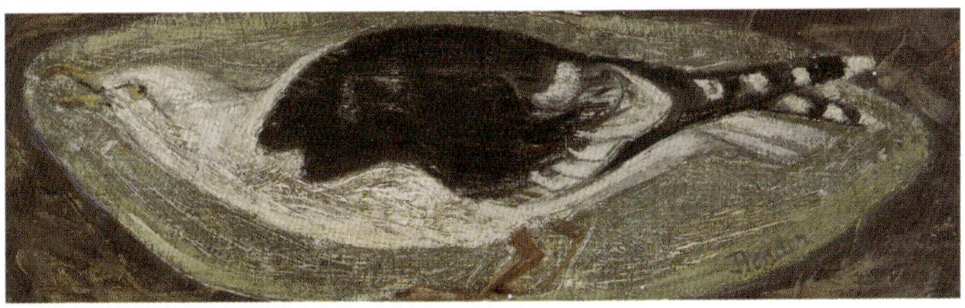

Untitled, c1950's, oil on board

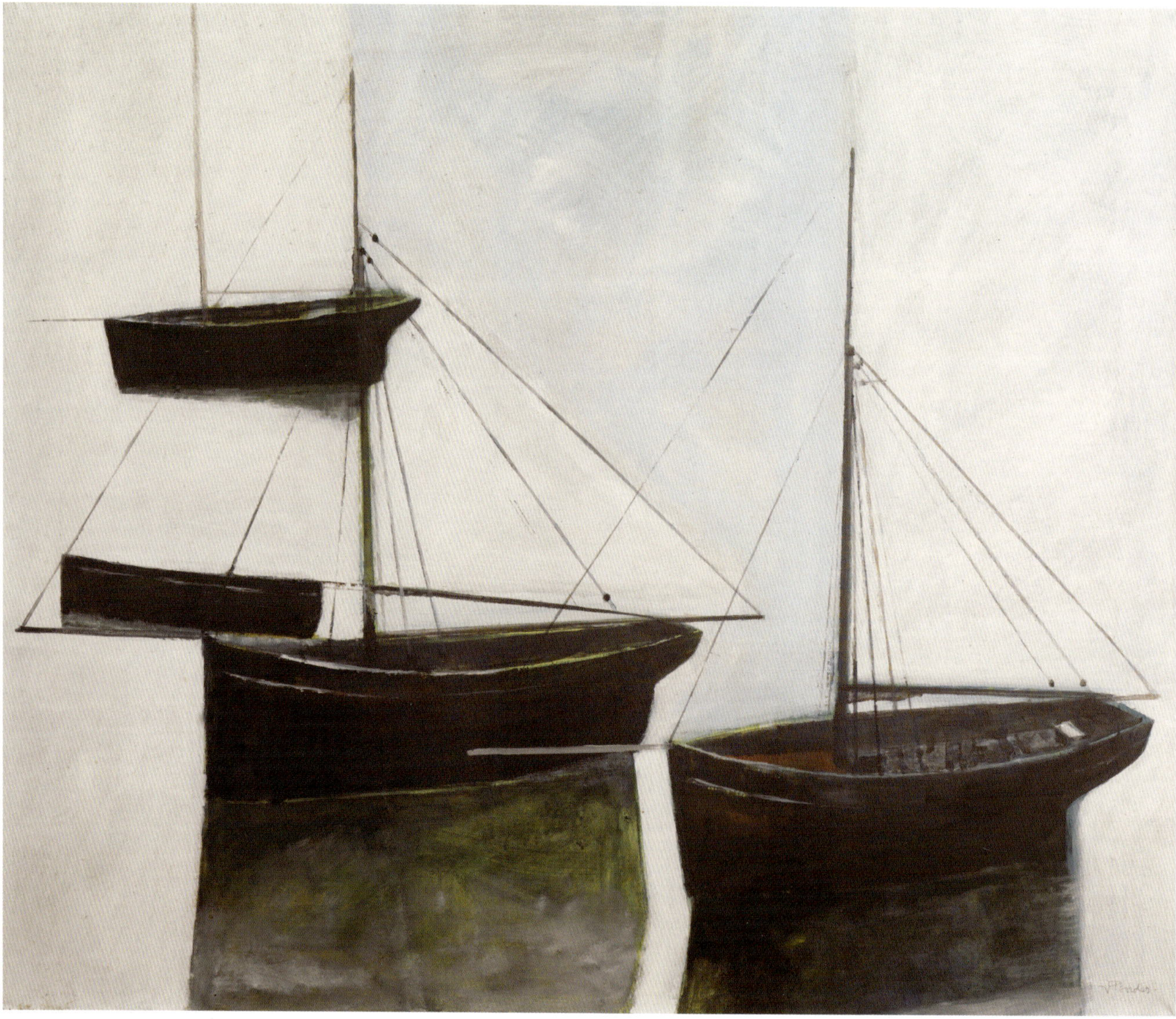

Untitled, oil on board